THE WAY AROUND

THE
WAY
AROUND

*A Field Guide
to Going Nowhere*

NICHOLAS
TRIOLO

MILKWEED EDITIONS

© 2025, Text by Nicholas Triolo
All rights reserved. Except for brief quotations in critical articles or reviews, no part of this book may be reproduced in any manner without prior written permission from the publisher: Milkweed Editions, 1011 Washington Avenue South, Suite 300, Minneapolis, Minnesota 55415.
(800) 520-6455
milkweed.org

Published 2025 by Milkweed Editions
Printed in Canada
Cover design by Mary Austin Speaker
Author photo by Rio Chantel
25 26 27 28 29   5 4 3 2 1
First Edition

Library of Congress Cataloging-in-Publication Data

Names: Triolo, Nicholas, author.
Title: The way around : a field guide to going nowhere / Nicholas Triolo.
Description: Minneapolis : Milkweed Editions, 2025. | Summary: "A memoir about circumambulating mountains as philosophical exploration"-- Provided by publisher.
Identifiers: LCCN 2024053238 (print) | LCCN 2024053239 (ebook) | ISBN 9781571313959 (hardcover) | ISBN 9781571317414 (ebook)
Subjects: LCSH: Triolo, Nicholas. | Runners (Sports)--United States--Biography. | Life.
Classification: LCC GV1061.15.T735 A3 2025 (print) | LCC GV1061.15.T735 (ebook) | DDC 796.42/092 [B]--dc23/eng/20241209
LC record available at https://lccn.loc.gov/2024053238
LC ebook record available at https://lccn.loc.gov/2024053239

Milkweed Editions is committed to ecological stewardship. We strive to align our book production practices with this principle, and to reduce the impact of our operations in the environment. We are a member of the Green Press Initiative, a nonprofit coalition of publishers, manufacturers, and authors working to protect the world's endangered forests and conserve natural resources. *The Way Around* was printed on acid-free 100% postconsumer-waste paper by Friesens Corporation.

For Mother

CONTENTS

Prologue   1

Round One: *Kailash*   11

Round Two: *Tamalpais*   59

Round Three: *Pit*   123

Epilogue   171

Notes   177

Additional Sources   185

Acknowledgments   189

Mystics claim that their ecstasy reveals to them a circular chamber containing a great circular book, whose spine is continuous and which follows the complete circle of the walls; but their testimony is suspect; their words, obscure. This cyclical book is God.

— Jorge Luis Borges, "The Library of Babel"

THE WAY AROUND

PROLOGUE

I live my life in widening circles
that reach out across the world.
I may not complete this last one
but I give myself to it.

I circle around God, around the primordial tower.
I've been circling for thousands of years
and I still don't know: am I a falcon,
a storm, or a great song?

— Rainer Maria Rilke, "Widening Circles"

In my early twenties, I decided to travel around the world. After saving for years, I embarked on a solo, one-year loop: Fiji, New Zealand, and Australia for the first six months, Hong Kong, China, Nepal, Southeast Asia, London, and Ireland for the second six months. In Kathmandu, I met up with my girlfriend, who had been conducting interviews in Tibetan refugee camps as part of her thesis research. Courtney picked me up at the airport and took me to Boudhanath, one of the city's most revered centers for the twenty thousand Tibetan refugees living in Nepal. We shouldered packs through a walkway and into a courtyard that stopped me in my tracks, where a 118-foot stupa stood before us, fluttering in thousands of prayer flags as people shuffled clockwise around its base.

"*Kora*," Courtney whispered in my ear. "They call this sort of walking *kora*. Learned about it in class the other day. Circumambulation."

The word *kora* had a better mouthfeel, coning my lips like the shape of the walk itself, but words mattered less than the action unfolding in front of us, maroon robes and shaved heads and pigeons flailing around a stupa set to a pair of half-open Buddha eyes painted on its whitewashed half-orb phallus. What spun at its base was unusual, legs and arms scissoring like some ill-choreographed ballet. Reaching the guesthouse required that we first pass through the walkers, and so, with our hands braided, Courtney tugged me forward into the whirl as people swarmed to our left and mantra-hummed to our right. Thousands of bodies everywhere. What I remember most is that the whole world seemed to spin, electrons orbiting their nucleus, some cosmic sensation of a universe whirling at once: We orbited the temple, which orbited the earth's core, which orbited the sun, which orbited the center of the Milky Way.

Everything turning, turning, turning.

We completed a first revolution. Then a second. Three rounds later, the two of us were ejected into the alley, dizzy in love. It would be several years before I learned that *kora* reflects a larger pattern of moving prayer, a several-thousand-year-old walking ritual practiced on every habitable continent and through every major world religion. I had never seen anything like it.

•••

Returning home, I couldn't shake that first encounter with *kora*. Something about it haunted me. I couldn't stop thinking about circles, about how our travels often aim toward another place, but, in the end, take us right back to where we started. In 2007, I moved to Portland, Oregon, and took a job in a downtown office with floor-to-ceiling windows above a sushi go-around that made everything smell of day-old tempura. Living and working in boxes was something I'd resisted my whole life, but began to settle into nicely. Cubicles. 401(k)s. Brown bag wellness seminars in windowless rooms with burned coffee and baby-blue nametags. I sought a counterbalance. That's when I discovered ultrarunning.

I remember first hearing the term ultrarunning—defined as any run extending beyond the 26.2-mile marathon distance—and thinking how ridiculous it sounded, some ego-masochistic charade for people too stupid to stop earlier. What began as a five-mile shuffle through Portland's Forest Park turned into two-hour runs, then four-hour runs, then all-day runs. During a heatwave in July, a friend and I ran thirty-four miles around the base of Mount Saint Helens, a continuation of my fixation with circuitous travel. Here, I was forced to rely on two feet to propel me around, not single-mindedly up. Mount Saint Helens is an active stratovolcano, its top blown off in 1980 by the equivalent force of twenty-five thousand Hiroshima bombs, so my introduction to encircling landscapes started here—a mountain without a summit.

Arriving to the car ten hours later, I vomited from heat exhaustion, and yet, as painful as it was, something clicked. Maybe it was committing to an adventure without the residue of summit conquest. Maybe it was encountering my own mortality. Or maybe it was something more mysterious, religious even—part endurance, part prostration, part mortification—a round of prayer at the feet of some headless god. In the end, I don't know exactly how I became obsessed with running long distances around mountains, but I knew I was hooked. These landscapes and routes had begun to work on me in subtle ways, leaving me to wonder:

How are the shapes we follow in life also shaping us?

•••

IN THE FOLLOWING YEARS, I RAN INCREASINGLY LONGER and faster, and that's when my body started eating itself. Once, after finishing a fifty-mile mountain race, I collapsed in the corner of a Conoco gas station bathroom, blacking out for thirty seconds. It happened again at a Subway in

New Mexico, midorder. I never told anyone. Fixated on the one-hundred-mile distance, my first attempt took twenty-six hours, a crossing of Oregon's Siskiyou Mountains with twenty thousand vertical feet of climbing. I lost consciousness at the finish line, revitalized by a team of nurses and smelling salts. The following year, a medical expert forced me to drop a second hundred-miler east of San Diego, after I'd filled a dixie cup to the brim with bloody urine the color of espresso. My kidneys were failing.

This did nothing to deter me, though it should have. I kept reaching. Raised by two professional tennis players in the San Francisco Bay Area taught me to always seek more, to push through the pain, hell-bent on accomplishment. *Do the reps. Commit to the work. Grind for your dreams.* Of course, such patterns were hardly unique to my family. This was something more systemic, defining self-worth by productivity and individual gain, myths of the never-enough and the always-more. Perpetual motion suited my personality, for stopping meant slowing, and slowing meant feelings, and feelings required work—it was easier to run.

Still, I knew that something wasn't right. In September, 2011, I found myself drawn into the Occupy Wall Street movement in Portland—the largest encampment outside New York City's Zuccotti Park. I joined in direct actions, dated a street artist, botched a hundred-foot banner drop during a protest, co-launched an anarchist affinity group. I wanted to know what the shape of a healthy human culture looked like when everyone had enough, whose primary aim wasn't to maximize profit but to widen our circumference of care.

After two months, Portland's police force swept away the occupation overnight, and the park returned to squares of fenced-off grass. One evening after work, I ran down to the park and completed ninety-nine laps around its perimeter, a private, if not contrived, act of solidarity for the 99 percent. I returned home four hours later, broken and limping, but happy. Moving in this way—not for some podium or linear act of achievement but in solidarity—seemed to align with the shape of Occupy's aims, a way to say farewell.

That same month, I qualified for the Western States 100-Mile Endurance Run, the Mount Everest of ultrarunning. Considered the world's most competitive hundred-mile foot race, the task was simple: run as fast as possible, point to point, reaching the finish line at any cost. The irony of ultrarunning as a path to ego-dissolution, while inviting me into this most egocentric competition, was inescapable. Something was going to break, either me or the growing dissonance.

On June 22, 2012, the gun fired at 5 a.m. Hundreds of headlamps charged west, one of them mine. Set near the summer solstice in Northern California, Western States is known for hot days, condensing an entire lifetime of emotion, euphoria, and anguish into one long run. Forty-three miles in, I arrived to the course's steepest climb, Devil's Thumb, where temperatures reached into the nineties. At mile sixty-two, a crew of family and friends met me for a food resupply, and I remember kissing my mother's cheek as it beaded in sweat and smelled of coconut sunscreen.

"Don't you ever do this again, promise me?" she whispered into my ear.

This was when things started to fall apart. Several runners began passing me and I felt the race slipping through my grip. I'd written "May the Beast Be Your Enlightenment" in Sharpie on my forearm as a mantra, but it was now a smeared Rorschach test. A sixteen-mile descent dropped down to the American River at mile seventy-five, where a raft shuttled me across. After submerging my body in its flow, triple-digit heat furnaced on the opposite shore, and everything began to seize up. Full-body cramps. Failing thoughts. Boredom on loop.

Ninety miles in, night fell as I followed the trail by headlamp, surrendering to the motion. The race's final mile passed through the town of Auburn over pavement radiating heat from the day as it led through a neighborhood to the finish—one victory lap around the high school track. Another runner funneled onto the finish line track the same time I did. I reached out for a hand-in-hand finish, but he wanted none of it and started to sprint. After covering one hundred miles on foot, I found myself in a full-kick finish, lungs afire, teeth grinding, lactic acid piston-fed and gurgling and coursing through every nerve as I reached out, extended limbs, knees, nose, whatever I could to finish ahead.

Finally, everything stopped.

One hundred miles.

Eighteen hours, fifty minutes.

Thirty-fourth place.

My dad scraped me off the track as everything started to convulse. Medical staff wrapped me in blankets, exhaustion and euphoria tangled in knots, and I blacked out, coming into focus an hour later in a Motel 6 bathtub filled with ice, a bottle of ibuprofen in one hand and two breakfast sandwiches in the other. Fascia taut as wire. Salt-crusted eyelids. Bloodshot eyes. Chafed penis. I'd reached a pinnacle of achievement, traveling farther in one day than I'd ever imagined going in a lifetime, but it also felt like I'd dug myself a grave.

Here, I was starting to understand that nothing much ever unfolds in linear fashion, that beginnings and endings are strange bedfellows, often swapping masks in a kind of sleight-of-hand exchange. What I didn't see coming was that the Western States race was more beginning than ending. Something had to die at that finish line in order for something else to be born. Sitting naked in the ice bath, simultaneously freezing and sweating, something cracked open. I vowed then that, as soon as my legs worked again, I would walk through that portal and find out what was on the other side.

...

THE WAY AROUND TRACES A PATH OF INQUIRY THAT I found on the other side of the portal. What follows are three circumambulations, a series of pilgrimages without destination set in three very different worlds, tracing three very different kinds of movement. Intimacy and attention, compassion and staying power, restraint and reverence—these were shapes I sought to embody, and it was indeed the body that proved to be my most trusted guide. From the western lip of the Tibetan plateau, tracing the spiritual headwaters of circumambulation, to a collision with the Beat countercultural West at the base of northern California's Mount Tamalpais, and ending with a self-designed lap around the rim of the largest Superfund site in the country, *The Way Around* charts a twenty-year devotion to a shape, a pattern of movement and stillness.

What are we encircling? What is encircling us? These questions brought me into an intimate sense of stillness-in-motion, a calm aliveness as storms of an unstable future build. What if surviving the perilous times ahead requires us to identify with a different trajectory, one that relies on questing *and* returning, achieving *and* relinquishing, one that centers mystery and humility as a way home? What if our survival demands a different story, which is to say a different shape, the shape of radical attention and restraint in pursuit of human and more-than-human flourishing? *The Way Around* carries these questions, each step an attempt to compose a love song underfoot, a storm song, a pilgrimage to nowhere and back again.

ROUND ONE | *Kailash*

Starlings circle in the sky,
conspiring,
together, and alone,
unspeakable journeys
into and out of the light.

— James Baldwin

ONE | *Arrival*

IT ONCE REQUIRED SEVERAL MONTHS OF OVERLAND travel to reach Lhasa, but these days you can arrive to Tibet's capital from anywhere in the world within forty-eight hours—that is, with the appropriate paperwork. The city stretches along floodplains of the Kyi Chu River, a waterway sutured in bridge and barley field downstream from an even larger arterial, the Yarlung Tsangpo, which runs 1,765 miles across the Tibetan Plateau—a landmass five times the size of France—its headwaters at the base of a lone mountain, considered by two billion people to be the most sacred mountain on the planet. This is where I'm headed.

When descending into Lhasa by plane, you can't miss the power lines and prayer flags. Half a million people live in the metropolitan area, inflated by another fifteen million annual visitors, mainly Han Chinese. Transmission lines flare from the city center to pass over mountains, trellised lines of watt and byte. As you draw closer to ground level, millions of prayer flags come into view, colored squares hung from every cleft and shingle appearing so numerous that one can't help but wonder how, or who, affixed them. Gale winds lift each prayer into bucking arcs and bows, and it must be understood that at some point these prayers will grow threadbare, loosen their grip, fall to the ground, and move no more.

At Lhasa's Gongkar Airport terminal, a Chinese boy screams uncontrollably after losing his parents in the crush of arriving travelers. Such countenance is likely less a function of abandonment than it is a manifestation of the barometric pressure blooming in his skull after arriving to an elevation of twelve thousand feet, direct from Beijing. Surrounding the child are cream-colored walls braced in steel and neon advertisements glowing beside windows that frame the Himalayan panorama outside. But this child cares nothing for angled steel and neon, nor for sacred mountains. He stands alone, exiled among a whiplash of light-headed businessmen and military recruits, and wails at top pitch, his crow-black hair buzzed to the scalp, his face red from crying, crimson like blood, like fury, like the color of his shirt, which reads, "Big Brothers Rule."

Arriving late in the morning, I am greeted by the Tibetan guides, Tashi and Tenzin. Younger than me, Tenzin's eyes are soft with mischief and acne-pocked cheeks. His jerky movements exaggerate a sense of hospitality, cheer as a counter to a more complicated truth under the skin. I'll be joining eighteen international academics, spiritual seekers, art historians, and adventurers, and I am by far the youngest. Uli is next in age, a marketing specialist in her mid-forties from Germany, with academic glasses and sand-colored hair grown to mid-ear. Her eruptive laugh leaves me in nagging silence if I don't laugh back. Macy, a retired children's yoga instructor from Seattle, smiles with her whole body, fragile, toothpicks for legs. Martin and Ann arrive next, a gorgeous couple from Switzerland, "Sauvignon and Scallops," I've begun to call them. Martin works in the financial sector and looks like he's made out of Kevlar. Ann, his wife, wears liberal amounts of makeup and tucks behind Martin's heft.

To my left is Rodney from Boulder, Colorado, a balding Buddhist practitioner and owner of a company that develops freeze-dried backpacking meals. Then there's Yvan and Nym from Bangkok. Yvan is busy filming the mountains, a British videographer living in Thailand wearing a newsboy hat and resembling a hunkier Pee-wee Herman. Nym is a prominent travel show personality—a female Anthony Bourdain of Thailand—with pigtails, a blue scarf, jet-black Ray-Bans, and tight pants. Ginny and Maddy both arrive from Maine, family members of our guide, Ian Baker. Ginny, his mother, wears a worn safari hat. Gray hair, big teeth. Maddy is Baker's cousin, a sarcastic high-elevation medical specialist. And then there is Pierre from Canada, a French language instructor and by far the most eccentric of the bunch, like your favorite, half-psychotic uncle.

"You into hockey, kid?" he asks after the group settles into our downtown guesthouse. Pierre's oversized red-and-blue Montreal jersey makes his bias clear. The man's eyes scan left to right before leaning closer, his breath smelling of rotting apricots. "You know, on the top of Mount Kailash sits Shiva. You'll see. This place is something else, something fucking else."

"Not your first time here?" I ask.

Pierre grins through a rack of shattered teeth. "Been here before, yeah. Unreal, surreal, *super* real," he says. "Traveled with a bunch of Hindus from India years ago. Way different this time, kid, way different." He gurgles the memory and rubs his palms as if planning a robbery.

From our guesthouse we step onto Beijing Road, a street congealed in bicycle, taxi, and rickshaw. Smells of pummeled kala jeera cumin meet faux Polo Sport meet the tang of petrol and untreated sewage while merchants canter along the sidewalk dodging tit-sagged mutts. Vendors twist elbows on their tables, kicking filled burlap sacks and picking at their teeth with packing wire, unimpressed by us tourists. Equally unamused are the four Chinese military officers stuffed in forest-green fatigues and cradling semiautomatics as we slide through security to enter the grounds of the Jokhang Monastery. Pierre turns his pockets inside out to show three flight stubs, a digital camera, mala beads, and a black 35mm film canister wrapped in tape.

Whitewashed walls mark the 1,300-year-old entrance as a cluster of Tibetans prostrate at its frontage below tapestries fringed in gold. Built in the seventh century by Tibet's founding king, Songtsen Gampo, the Jokhang features kilometer-long murals with lavish courtyards and perhaps the most precious relic for all Tibetans set like a seed in the middle—a four-foot statue of Jowo Rinpoche. Said to have been blessed by the Buddha himself, the artifact arrived by wooden cart in 641 CE, carved by Vishwakarma, Indian god of craftsmanship, and transported from China by Princess Wencheng, one of Gampo's many wives. The statue became severed in half during the Cultural Revolution in the 1960s, only to be festooned back to life in gilt metal, semiprecious stones, and pearls. Tibetans now hold the statue as close to their identity as anything. Two halves made whole.

Pierre and I stand at the gates flanked by ten-foot towers of burning sage, *riwo sangchö*. A cobblestone path follows the monastery's outer walls where a flow of walkers follows the path around. We wait for the appropriate moment to enter the stream and, amid mumbled prayer, join in their revolutions.

"*Kora*," Pierre whispers as we walk, summoning memories of my first encounter in Nepal with this practice that buoys exiled Tibetans to their homeland and cultural identity. Now, nearly a decade later, I witness this circumambulation from within, as if I'd stepped into some inverted center of gravity. Pierre reminds me that Tibetans practice *kora* around sacred sites, human-built or otherwise—temples, homes, mountains, lakes, even other people—to embody the cyclical nature of life and death, samsara, or reincarnation; to conduct a cleansing; to honor the dead; to gain merit and happiness. *Kora* can also serve as something more social, a way to gather, exercise, gossip. This one-mile circuit around Lhasa's Barkhor neighborhood is the most worn of four major routes in the city—the others being Nangkhor, Tsekhor, and Lingkhor—all sharing the common suffix *-khor*, Sanskrit for "circulating breath" or "magic circle." But what brings me here is a much larger magic circle, a *kora* nine hundred miles west and thirty-two miles around the base of the world's most sacred geological feature in all of Bon, Hindu, Buddhist, and Jain cosmology: Mount Kailash.

Kang Rinpoche in Tibetan, Kailash is a 21,778-foot Himalayan outlier, an aberrant tooth in a jawbone of the Gangdise Range, where its lake basins are headwaters to four of the world's most consequential rivers: the Karnali, Indus, Sutlej, and Brahmaputra. Seven hundred and fifty million people—double the population of the United States—depend on fresh water from these four rivers alone. Many refer to Tibet as the planet's "Third Pole" because of its forty-six thousand glaciers, the largest freshwater repository outside Earth's polar reserves. Just as Jowo Rinpoche rests chambered in the middle of the Jokhang, Kailash sits in divinity as a cosmological water tower for billions.

Mount Kailash is often referred to as an axis mundi, an umbilical conduit connecting soil to sky, a tent pole to prop up the heavens, a navel around which all of Hindu-Buddhist cosmology whirls. Tens of thousands of pilgrims arrive annually to follow the thirty-two-mile path around its base. The walk takes several days, though some complete the circuit in just one. The most pious perform full-body prostrations around the mountain, some starting in Lhasa and prostrating nine hundred miles along the highway for several months in their approach. Each footstep around is thought to keep the mountain from flying away, for the Buddha is said to be its inaugural pilgrim, securing Kailash with four steps placed in each cardinal direction so the gods wouldn't one day decide to lift the mountain up and take it elsewhere. This is what *kora* seeks to recreate with every step, while never forgetting the mountain's cardinal rule—no one is allowed to touch the summit.

...

AFTER THREE DAYS OF HEADACHES AND ACCLIMATIZATION in Lhasa, our expedition bags pile to the ceiling of the guesthouse lobby as Tenzin and his crew ferry them to two vans and a Land Rover. The two-week journey starts today, an itinerary that leads us west through Shigatse, Tibet's second largest city, before camping along the highway until Darchen, gateway to Kailash, where our team will embark on a four-day walking circuit around the mountain. From there, the convoy will drive to the western edge of the plateau, near Kashmir, to spend time among the ruins of the Guge Kingdom, before returning to Lake Manasarovar and back to Lhasa.

Ian Baker, our main guide, sinks into the hotel lobby couch. His khaki vest covers a white travel shirt set against coal-dark eyes and shoulder-length hair that recedes in front but bunches in the back, topped with a worn brimmed hat. At sixty years old, Baker exudes a youthful celebrity aura—Indiana Jones, meet John Malkovich—while a British accent clings to a few of his words, residue from doctoral studies at Oxford and London College. In the morning glow, Baker appears confident yet unfulfilled, the sort of gaze an explorer of the deep sea might have after too many days beneath the surface.

I first encountered Baker's book *The Heart of the World* in 2006, the same year this whole fixation with circuitous travel began during my trip around the world. It chronicles a harrowing expedition through the Pemako region that straddles southeastern Tibet and northeastern India through the world's deepest gorge, in search of a real-life Shangri-La. As an obsessive seeker in my late teens, I found Baker's writing and work to embody the type of wayfaring intellectual I aspired to become, someone who traveled to faraway places but who never fixated on outdoor pursuit as an end in itself. Baker descended into some of the planet's most remote underworlds in search of the human heart in courtship with the heart of the world. This was something I sought most, though I had few mentors to show the way, to live guided by curiosity, not simply collecting experiences.

A decade later, he resurfaced one evening during graduate school, where I was researching Buddhism, ecology, and pilgrimage, and all roads led to Kailash. Following my initial exposure to *kora*, I had begun mapping circumambulation sites around the world, and this mountain kept tugging at my imagination. I daydreamed of getting to its base one day, and to my surprise, I found that Baker himself was leading a group around the mountain the following year. In that moment, something became clear. I had to join him, no matter the cost.

Traveling to Kailash made sense for several reasons. This mountain was the most evocative land feature I had ever witnessed in photos, making my eyes swell with tears and my palms clam up. I was also drawn in largely by the fact that its summit was forbidden. The fact that there was an off-limits peak worshipped by a third of humanity and tucked deep in the Himalaya felt subversive in a way I couldn't fully understand until seeing it firsthand. Walking around, as opposed to up, seemed to gesture at a ritual of embodied restraint during times of hyperactive globalization and take-and-grab economics. Here, I felt drawn to this mountain, to visit its antisummit and proceed to do what everyone else was doing—leave it the hell alone.

The third reason for traveling to Kailash was pure self-indulgence. What I know about the origins of the Kailash pilgrimage is that the first human to chart a way around was the Tibetan sage Gotsampa in the thirteenth century, an itinerant musician brought up in abject poverty. It's said that, after his father died, Gotsampa had no choice but to turn to Buddhism, by then the dominant religion on the plateau. His teacher prescribed a solo mountain retreat for the monk, and so, at age twenty-five, Gotsampa departed for Kailash, following his master's advice. Guided by a female *dri*, or yak, he started to walk clockwise around the base over several days, taking refuge in caves and lashed by foul weather, but always keeping the mountain to his right. Whenever Gotsampa lost the path, *dikinis*, elusive alpine fairies, revealed themselves to light the way. Word spread about Kailash's powers, and the pilgrimage became a focal point of convergence for Bonpo, Hindu, Jain, and Buddhist ascetics.

When the first Italian Jesuit missionaries arrived to the region in the seventeenth century, they set their sights on the remote mountain, passed along through stories and maps. Father Antonio Andrade was the first European to witness Kailash while spreading the word of God along the Silk Road and other Asian trading routes, though he never reached the mountain. The first European to reach its base was another Italian missionary, Ippolito Desideri, in 1715, who succumbed to snow blindness and retreated from his attempt:

> Kailash is a mountain of excessive height and great circumference, always enveloped in clouds, covered in snow and ice, and most horrible, barren, steep and cold. The Tibetans walk devoutly around the base of this mountain which takes several days, and they believe this will bring them great indulgences. Owing to the snow on the mountain my eyes became so inflamed that I well nigh lost my sight.

No other Western explorer braved the pilgrimage for another two hundred years, until Swedish geographer Sven Hedin arrived during a series of trips to Central Asia. On his third attempt (1905–1908), Hedin entered the Himalaya after first being denied access to Lhasa years prior. Following a visit to Tibet's Panchen Lama in Shigatse, Hedin tacked west in search of headwaters for India's Brahmaputra and Indus Rivers, but Kailash was too tempting to pass up, and in 1907, he completed the first circuit of any foreigner.

"At every turn I could stand still in astonishment," wrote Hedin, "for this valley is one of the grandest and most beautiful in its wildness that I have ever seen."

In the twentieth century, Western mountaineering expeditions penetrated deeper into the Himalaya to tackle the world's highest peaks. Despite warnings, a first Kailash ascent attempt came in 1926, when British mountaineer Hugh Ruttledge studied its north face, estimating the climb would reach to about twenty thousand feet. Luckily, he never followed through. Colonel R. C. Wilson, another British expeditioner, considered the southern ridge but ran out of time as a harsh winter closed in and he was forced to retreat. Australian climber Herbert Tichy expressed interest in the summit, too, but after asking a local lama for advice, the lama responded: "Only a man entirely free of sin could climb Kailash, and, actually, you wouldn't even need to climb, as you'd just turn yourself into a bird and fly to the top." Tichy was not free of sin and the lama left him spooked, so he declined the bid.

It wasn't until 1985 when a summit attempt of Kailash was seriously considered, this time by Italian-born mountaineer Reinhold Messner, known widely for the first ascent of Mount Everest without supplemental oxygen. Counter to Tibet's wishes, China gave Messner express permission and yet, after much deliberation and public outcry, he declined at the last minute, stating: "If we conquer this mountain, then we conquer something in people's souls." The last known attempt to summit Kailash was in 2001, when Spanish climber Jesus Martinez Novas sought to broadcast a message of peace from the top, but, after global outrage, he called it off. Rumors suggest Chinese mountaineers have attempted to reach the top, but nothing has been documented. To this day, the summit remains untouched, except for by Chakrasamvara, the Circle of Bliss, Parvati, and Shiva the Destroyer.

TWO | *En Route*

OUR CONVOY BEGINS ITS FOUR-DAY JOURNEY WEST TO Kailash, leaving Lhasa to connect with the major highway that tracks upriver along the Yarlung Tsangpo. Passing through multiple checkpoints, we follow a train line that cuts straight, built by the Chinese to link Lhasa with Shigatse. This, along with the paved strip of highway we follow, contrasts the surrounding landscape, through steep, gray-beige canyons and broad valleys cribbed in by mountains, mostly bare of greenery at this elevation. The quality of light hides nothing in its conspiring with Earth and sky, a charade of elements that demands a different kind of attention, one that tweaks your neck to fully honor all that's unfolding, superlative landscapes and glacier-fed green rivers without end.

Before spilling off this plateau on its way to India, the Yarlung Tsangpo River that we follow drops eight thousand vertical feet south and east through canyons before being renamed the Brahmaputra. Here, it careens through gorges twice as deep as the Grand Canyon—those visited by Ian Baker in *The Heart of the World*—before reaching India, where the river takes a major hairpin turn called the "Great Bend" and generates tremendous power, sixty gigawatts of power. Baker tells me that the Chinese are currently building the largest megadam on the planet at this bend, bigger than the Three Gorges Dam, the hydroelectric project that displaced

1.3 million people and destroyed entire ecosystems. China is, by far, the biggest dam builder in the world, and Tibet possesses enormous hydroelectric potential. Two-thirds of the eighty-seven thousand Chinese dams are located on or around the plateau, and there are believed to be two dozen more dams scheduled for this waterway.

Heading upriver, our van rattles across speed bumps to signal an upcoming military checkpoint. A Chinese soldier stands erect at the side of the road. He doesn't face west toward Kailash, but angles east toward the Great Bend and his employer, Father Beijing. The driver downshifts, but the soldier's posture holds: white helmet, white straps, white belt, all aligned with uncanny precision, a rifle following the seam of his right pant leg. As we approach the guard, our driver curses under his breath and hits the gas because, upon closer inspection, the soldier isn't made of flesh and blood, but plaster and concrete. All along the highway, the Chinese military has placed hundreds of these fake soldiers as deterrents—security scarecrows—as well as tens of thousands of real soldiers.

Baker doesn't flinch. From the copilot's seat, he stares at the road ahead while his mother, Ginny, sits behind him. Earlier that day, she had shared more about her son. She told me that Ian, when he was ten, used to scrape gum from the bottoms of park benches and sample them, one by one, and that he would steal Valium from the family dog's prescription and try fistfuls for himself. She blamed Baker's intensity on a demanding New England boarding school and spoke fondly of his father, who would hum Pete Seeger folk songs and take him sailing. After completing graduate and doctoral work at Middlebury College, Oxford, and Columbia, Baker moved to Nepal to lead research expeditions, for what sustained him most were the world's hidden parts, *beyuls*, specifically the esoteric practices of Himalayan tantra. In 2000, *National Geographic* named Baker one of the top seven explorers of the millennium. On one expedition to the remote Yang Sang of northern India, he spent several weeks with Indigenous communities.

"These tribespeople wore collars of tiger teeth and daggers that touched the floor," Baker tells me. "The shamans were all female too. And to celebrate foreigners—which never happened because there weren't any—the whole village went hunting for rats. We gorged on barbequed rats."

In 2008, everything shifted. While Baker was away from his Kathmandu home, Nepali authorities raided his place, where he'd been living for fourteen years, and discovered one hundred and twenty-one artifacts—tiger skins, pelts, statues, tangkas, and other rare items. As a guide and fellow for the National Geographic Society and Smithsonian Institute, Baker's reputation was on the line, a warrant issued for his arrest. His explanation? "Completely false." Baker claimed he'd been protecting these items from being destroyed, that the Nepali heist was a last-ditch effort by the royal police to steal what they could before losing power. "You see this great legacy of culture and wildlife being allowed to rot, to go to waste. I was trying to prevent that." He escaped to Bangkok, where he lives today.

Baker's drive for ecocultural preservation seems far more plausible than wild pelt trafficking, yet despite being a leading scholar of comparative literature and a lifelong practitioner of Tibetan Buddhism, and despite having written several books—two in collaboration with His Holiness the Fourteenth Dalai Lama—my first impressions are that he appears cynical, rightly detesting China's conquest of

Tibet while criticizing Buddhism's lackluster responses to environmental and social concerns. On the other hand, he proves to be generous in sharing his authority of Tibet's storied landscape. For hours, Baker pines over the intricacies of Tibetan tangkas and artifacts as we stop at monasteries along the way, transmitting much of what he'd picked up over his many trips here, including a decades-long intimacy with circumambulation.

As we travel to the west, Baker tells me that *kora* is, at its essence, one of the great remaining embodiment practices of depersonalization, for performing these circuits heightens the potential to transcend ordinary consciousness, if one's motivation is pure. Around Kailash, whenever a pilgrim crosses the route's high point—18,500-foot Dolma La Pass—pain has the potential to disrupt the ego. "After making the pass, it's possible for one to no longer experience the bodily hardship in a personalized way," he says. "You may transcend *ego*centric consciousness and attain a more *eco*centric view, where you become part of a tremendous whole. Any narrowing or limiting of the self can dissolve by way of this circling."

His eyes pass from smolder to bonfire as the topic arouses him, while my eyes bumble in their sockets, unable to integrate this abstraction. What he says makes intellectual sense, and yet I still have no idea how this walk might actually dissolve me. It all feels so distant, something I've only known in photographs.

"Circling is what planets do, you see?" says Baker. "And that, in the ultimate sense, is what *kora* does. It's as if we are surrendering, participating in a voluntary, intentional way, into a kind of cosmic order, an order where planets rotate, the solar system rotates, we rotate. The . . ."

Zheep zheep zheep!

An alarm from the van's dashboard interrupts Baker's ruminations. Plugged into the cigarette lighter is a speed governor issued by the Chinese government that chirps at the driver whenever he exceeds the limit. Pierre cackles from the backseat. Our group has only been together for a week now and already Pierre is wearing on me, on Baker, on the others, his hockey jersey smelling of sweat, his legs spread to take up as much space as possible.

"If you look a bit deeper," Baker continues, "we're actually spinning in the cosmos right now at a tremendous speed, both circumnavigating the sun while at the same time spinning on our own axis. Everything circles."

"So why is it so important for Tibetans to perform *kora* together?" I ask.

"It's important to join others in *kora* because we all slip into a stream, a current, movement with shared intentionality," he explains. "In a certain sense, everyone is going around the mountain with the same aim—to reflect and transform their lives, overcoming something that limits us, something that holds us back."

Zheep zheep zheep!

The speed governor sounds off again, making the skin on Baker's face pull tight around his nose. The driver decelerates and spritzes dark juice out the window through gapped teeth. Pierre froths from the back and scratches his groin. Uli, the German marketing specialist, plugs in her earbuds to watch the plateau roll along undisturbed. Baker's mother Ginny sits tall, calm, while Baker mutters something chummy in Tibetan to the driver, who ignores him.

...

AFTER FOUR DAYS OF CAMPING ALONG THE G219 HIGHWAY toward Darchen, I catch my first glimpse of Kailash during a bathroom break on the side of the highway. The mountain rises like a beacon, fifty miles in the distance, a shark fin cutting through Himalayan highland like the volcanoes dotting the Pacific Northwest horizon that invited me into these earlier orbits. The reveal catches me off guard and I collapse into a pile of emotion, as if I were looking into a newborn's eyes for the first time—no land feature had ever done that to me.

The more I learn about circumambulation's origins, the more I understand why Kailash drew me to my knees, as the beginnings of humans walking in ritual circles reaches back at least five thousand years, its earliest known expression thought to be a kind of solar mimicry. In 3000 BCE, accounts emerged in Egypt of circumambulation as worship to the sun deity Ra, "the walking god...the great walker who goes (daily) over the same course...Thou stridest over the heaven, being glad of heart...his strides are long as he lifteth up his legs," modeling the sun's return each day. Similar evidence surfaced in Bihar, northern India, where temples were built in orientation to Surya, the Hindu sun god. But there's one mythic origin story that really caught my attention.

In the earliest years of Hindu's Vedic period—1750 BCE to 500 BCE—adepts also incorporated circular walking, *pradakshina* or *parikrama*, to reenact an old myth where the sage Narada visited Lord Shiva and his wife Parvati, both of whom lived atop Kailash. The man was curious which of their two sons, Ganesh and Kartikeya, was more intelligent, so he proposed they find out through a competition where the victor would receive a luscious mango pulled from the sage's satchel, a fruit to induce divine wisdom for whoever bit into it first. The two sons fought over who was most deserving, until their parents halted the quibbling with a duel: Each would perform three laps around the world. The first one home would win the fruit of wisdom.

Kartikeya, god of war, took to the road and swirled around the world on a peacock, dressed in flamboyant clothing, armor, and weaponry. Ganesh, an elephant with only a mouse for a vehicle, knew he stood no chance against his brother and decided to stay home and romp three circles around his parents instead, proclaiming that all of the world's truths were contained right here, right now. There's no need to seek wisdom outside ourselves, for divinity rests like a precious jewel inside our own bosoms. Shiva and Parvati were so touched they awarded Ganesh the mango, to the displeasure of his wayfaring brother, and many today are said to be retracing Ganesh's prints as they perform *kora*, or *pradakshina*—odd numbers for female deities, even numbers for male counterparts.

When Buddhism emerged in India around 500 BCE, Hindu traditions and rites informed many of its earliest practices. Circumambulation was one of them, spreading quickly afield and found all over the Buddhist world today. On Japan's Shikoku Island, a one-thousand-mile clockwise pilgrimage links eighty-eight Buddhist shrines for one very long walk. If monks start the circuit but do not finish, they are expected to skewer a sword through their stomach; in fact, they are said to carry swords with them as they walk, so as to not lose sight of the lethal stakes. *Kinhin* is a common Zen practice, in which practitioners walk the perimeter of a meditation room following seated zazen. In Central Java, Indonesia, pilgrims spiral upward over one hundred vertical feet to pass through several levels of Buddhist cosmology engraved in stone on the world's largest Buddhist monument, the ninth-century Borobudur

Stupa, ascending from the world of lowly desires up through illusory form, and then finally to its apex, formlessness.

The beginnings of circular pilgrimage might be seen as one of the earliest known forms of cosmomimicry, walking in patterns as heavenly bodies first appeared to have wheeled along the night sky, east to west, clockwise when peering south, simultaneously drawn in by gravity while pulled outward and around in kinship. Circumambulation seems to have grown from a simple method of reverence and grounding, a way both outward and inward: a merging with God and exchange of solipsism for a wider unified field, if also an inward homecoming to the Self. These opposing drives may not be as separate as they appear, for the encircling pilgrim is courting some unknowable core, some mystery or god, a forever unknowable at the center, and this courtship is said to widen the circumference of Self, of belonging, two forces working together as lovers might.

...

AFTER REACHING DARCHEN, THE GROUP HAS GROWN road-rattled, fixated on the destination, but beaten down by all that's already been traversed. Having followed the "Friendship Highway" to its terminus with the Yarlung Tsangpo River, our convoy covered a thousand miles, squeezing over several sixteen-thousand-foot passes pocked in military checkpoints—I've counted twenty-three—many with real soldiers and real guns and real hours-long delays. Despite stop-and-go surveillance, oceans of alpine grasses spread in every direction alongside fields of barley and yellow rapeseed, while rock-strewn canyons in the distance invite the eye farther and deeper into unfenced unknowns. Tibet plays with scale at every turn, a constant game of hide-and-seek, only to reappear again under scudding clouds to blur space and complicate perception. This plateau will outlast our violence and our gods.

Darchen offers little to soften the road calluses. At fifteen thousand feet, this village was once an important waypoint for nomads and herders, but now sprawls into unchecked commercialism, tourism, and forgotten sewage. Darchen sounds like *darshan*: a sacred moment of witness, positioned with front-row seats for us to view Kailash at its immediate north. The town's three main avenues form a trident, each prong tapering north into bad weather that conceals the mountain. Perhaps this is Kailash teaching its first lesson: Anytime we attach ourselves to a perceived destination of truth, it skitters away. Nothing so simple reveals itself.

A driving rain reveals itself as we arrive, just in time for Baker to learn that the guesthouse he reserved months ago no longer exists. Wiped clean off the map. Our group relocates to the only available place big enough to accommodate eighteen guests, a collapsing row of cinder block barracks. Tenzin unloads bags into the middle of the parking lot as the group starts to drift away. The Swiss couple, Sauvignon and Scallops, needs a pilsner. Nym, the Thai television personality, needs more B-roll. Rodney needs a hot shower. Macy, the children's yoga instructor, asks where she can find lotion. No lotion in Darchen. Demands stack up until Baker, after repeated attempts to keep everyone together, erupts.

"Stop!" he says. "Stop exactly where you are." Duffels pile atop duffels in the rain, all the baggage we've brought now exposed. His face beet red and exhausted, Baker demands that everyone follow his lead as the rain turns to a downpour. *Kang Rinpoche*, our mountain compass to the north, is nowhere to be seen.

THREE | *Kora*

TODAY BEGINS OUR FOUR-DAY WALK AROUND KAILASH. An unclaimed human tooth stained in plaque leans on the windowsill next to three flies rotting belly-up in a pile of flaked skin and dust from the room's constant cycling of guests. Cinder block walls slopped in white paint offer an illusion of hygiene as five plywood beds clog a room made for two. Morning fatigue combines high elevation with having to avoid paint chips dislodged from the ceiling after the two Indian pilgrims next door grunted through sex for the second time, using our shared wall as leverage. Outside, Tenzin prepares instant coffee, toast, and fried eggs that crackle in rapeseed oil while everyone prepares for the first leg: twelve miles up the Lha Chu River Valley.

Despite thin walls and leftover teeth, I find the guesthouse pleasant, even after sharing a head-piercingly cold shit at dawn with an elder yak herder who squatted next to me in the latrine, so close that the sides of our knees grazed as he smiled at me, toothless above the open-air earthen hole splattered with blood and feces. Perhaps the incisor in my room was his.

Most of our group traveled here in pairs except for Pierre and me, so we were asked to share rooms, and he is up before me. Bags packed. Meditations and mantras completed. Pierre takes the opportunity to tell me his story, how he was born in 1958, how he grew up next to a comic book store on Main Street in Rivière-du-Loup, Quebec, how his "young and dumb" parents wasted no time expressing hatred for each other through physical violence. Pierre's father, Audre, was a compulsive drunk and went from inconsistent to sloppy to nonexistent. His parents separated and left him with his grandparents, who would leave the toddler in a backyard playpen over humid Quebec summer days, only to return and find him singing songs to garter snakes that gathered around his pen.

Pierre's grandparents were good-natured, though, and he received a decent childhood on their watch. Grandpa was a freight train engineer; Grandma, a tough countrywoman made of nickel and hardwood who dropped school for farm work. Pierre spent his early years turning to hockey and fights, pulped regularly by bullies. His mother would resurface from time to time while his father kept away—he remembers seeing him only twice during his childhood. The first time, he arrived unannounced and drunk at his grandparent's front door. Grandpa blew his top and demanded he leave. The second time, he arrived dressed as a sailor and convinced them to let him take Pierre to the toy store, where he bought him a purple plastic water pistol. Then, radio silence.

At nineteen, Pierre hitchhiked through Mexico, managed ten thousand sheep on a New Zealand wool farm, and eventually circled back to Quebec, where he met his wife Regina and started a family and career teaching English at a community college. On January 20, 1992, Regina gave birth to a baby girl, Rebecca. Rebecca grew up healthy, with two parents present and available. No drunken drop-ins. No purple guns. No snake songs. No fistfights. Rebecca loved music some and volleyball more, normal activities for a teenage girl, until she was fifteen, when she started to develop mysterious health complications.

And this is where Pierre's sharing skids to a halt. He leaps ahead to present day, tucking back into Buddhist esoterica, a pivot that leaves me forgetting about Kailash for a moment, about Vajrayana this or tantric that. I'd traveled seven thousand miles to reach the base of the world's most sacred mountain and now all I can think about is this strange man's sick daughter.

• • •

BEFORE WE START THE FIRST LEG OF THE WALK, TENZIN and I sip coffee and exchange jokes in patchy English. The previous night, he'd taken me to an open-air billiards hall, where we squatted under a single crooked halogen light to watch yak herders battle with unblinking precision.

Today's route departs clockwise from Darchen, flat and kind to unqualified lungs, curling north to follow the Lha Chu, where waterfalls tumble from bare cliffs hundreds of vertical feet to carve a wide-mouthed valley, inviting us deeper. I want for these first steps to feel circular, but the path seems to extend straight ahead. This section brings to mind my first mountain circuit around Mount Saint Helens, where it felt similarly linear.

Few pilgrims walk this morning, unusual for the Year of the Wood Horse, Buddha's birth year. To perform *kora* on a Wood Horse year is to double-stamp one's karmic passport. We pass Tarboche, the ceremonial prayer pole first raised in 1681 and resurrected annually during the Saga Dawa festival. Baker expected hundreds of Tibetans to be congregating here, but today there are none. Fenced off. A Chinese security guard appears out of nowhere to hurry us along. The guard is an extension of a long and torturous history of Chinese occupation in Tibet, something I can hardly understand, a history of occupation in search of land and resources.

Here's what I know: In 1950, one year after Mao Zedong established the People's Republic of China, he sent forty thousand troops from the People's Liberation Army (PLA) to invade Tibet. In the wake of the Second World War, Chinese authorities were interested mainly in the region's bountiful resources and its favorable geopolitical position with India. Tibet's spiritual and political leader, the Fourteenth Dalai Lama, then a teenager, attempted peaceful negotiations with the Chinese for several years, which amounted to nothing. Pressure mounted between waves of incoming Chinese settlers and Tibetan residents, and it peaked on March 10, 1959, when protests turned into armed conflict between Tibetans and the PLA. Over a quarter million Tibetans were said to form a buffer around the Potala Palace, where the Dalai Lama lived, to protect him from being kidnapped or assassinated. In all, eighty thousand were killed during the Tibetan Uprising. The Dalai Lama escaped to India, where the Tibetan government-in-exile works to this day. In the early 1960s, Mao's Great Leap Forward—a failed centralization program to transform agrarian China—led to wholesale famine and an estimated thirty million deaths, as well as the decade-long Cultural Revolution, a campaign that destroyed many traditional Tibetan monasteries and relics and triggered three decades of brutal occupation and genocide, resulting in the deaths of a million Tibetans and 150,000 more forced into exile.

"They are feeling particularly threatened by Tibetan gatherings this year," Baker says as we walk the first mile together. "Permits were severely restricted. We barely got ours." He shares that the Chinese are currently making plans to pave a road around Kailash for tour buses to encircle the mountain in an air-conditioned afternoon.

Along this section of the path, trash chokes a drainage ditch carved by snowmelt:

> instant noodle wrappers
> mini cans of Red Bull, gold-rimmed with two beasts, heads butting
> hundreds of plastic water bottles
> one, no two bloody tampons
> toilet paper, soiled
> pink paper prayer squares looking bruised
> corroded car battery
> manila envelope with official address from Beijing
> gray cotton sweatshirt, ripped
> box of plastic syringes, one left

Beside it leans a blue garbage barrel with Tibetan, Chinese, and English translations: "Treasure the Environment, No Littering."

Before arriving, I imagined Kailash as a mountain unfouled. This delusion embossed its jewel into some idea, a fixed place where my imagination could feast on it from afar. Now, the territory unspools with competing narratives and cosmologies, and to chart the birth of Kailash requires a much deeper, downward gaze, down past this flutter of rubbage at my feet, past even the Chinese occupation and into plate dynamics and magma.

One hundred seventy-five million years ago, the supercontinent of Pangea split, and what would form the Indian subcontinent piled north through an ancient Tethys Ocean to burrow under the Eurasian plate, uplifting to form the great Himalaya. Following the last known mass extinction, the Cretaceous-Paleogene (K-T), sixty-six million years ago—caused by an asteroid that struck near Mexico's Yucatan Peninsula, blotting out the sun and killing off much of the megaflora and fauna—this period also experienced high levels of seismic activity, which produced new vents in the Earth's crust to further speed up the warming, like west-central India's Deccan Traps. As the Indian landmass continued shoving its way north into Eurasia, these cracks released enormous amounts of gas, compounding an already warming world and winking out maladaptive species. The Tethys Ocean disappeared with the collision, developing a continental berm of mountains that sequestered all previous coastline farther inland. This trapped marine life inland, too, drying up to form the sweeping, high-elevation plains we traverse today.

Kailash's geological origin story is one of a misfit, exiled north from its cousins to the south, Everest and Annapurna. The mountain's idiosyncratic shape is due to wide-scale faulting and folding of metamorphosed sedimentary rock and its melding with igneous granitic deposits. Without samples from the summit, geologists agree that what composes Kailash's high point is what's called a "roof pendant," a metasedimentary cap resting atop a colossal base of granite below. Whereas Mount Saint Helens's peak was blown off altogether, the summit of Kailash is turned upside down, an underworld exposed to the upperworld.

Summits are never where we think they are.

...

THE SECOND MORNING OF THE *KORA* SNIPS COLD AS BLADES as two minor hills cradle the lone massif of Kailash in the middle. Snowdrift plumes from its shoulders like a funeral pyre while a northern flank arcs in an avalanche chute, falling thousands of feet to the valley floor where I sit at dawn. The Himalayan half-oval resembles a 21,778-foot tombstone or three million panels of corrugated iron brazed together and placed on end, seeming to bend physics to shift Earth's gravity, where everything now orbits its base. Part of me still can't believe this is real, this unending granite wall erupting before me, a vertical god cut from below and reaching four vertical miles above sea level.

We've covered eight miles and camped here to acclimate before attempting the 18,500-foot Dolma La Pass tomorrow. I look up from 17,100 feet, observing this peak forbidden by Tibetans, Hindu, Jain, and Bon, as first light bleeds from crown to slope to base. My eyeballs throb in their sockets as they trace the heft of its sedimentary roof pendant perforating the sky to set everything beneath it in motion. I can't stop wondering what it would be like to stand on that summit at first light. Unlike Mount Saint Helens, that original headless mountain god, here I can imagine the ting of an ice axe, hear the friction of synthetic expedition gear, and stand hypoxic at its apex as firstborn slivers of sunlight arrive, beams fired from ninety million miles away to meet a chapped face as I peer down onto the Lha Chu River, onto our cluster of fifteen yellow tents. We do not belong up here. We are not gods.

I follow a dab of strawberry-colored light as it ripens the upper slope, rock chinked like a staircase for Shiva and Parvati. My body shivers with dueling awe and exile; home never felt so far away. Inside the mess tent, Tenzin pokes at breakfast with a wooden ladle—daal and chapatti. The smell is familiar; we've been eating it every day for a week. I sit alone and stare at the mountain. *Fight the burning eyes, forget your throbbing head, your distended fingers. Don't blink; you'll regret it. Look hard.* Movement begins to overtake the silence: pilgrims, then tent zippers, then puffing kettles, then the bell-clank of hungry yaks. Tenzin shuffles toward me now, his face acne-cratered and gorgeous. He holds two cups of tea gobbed in butter and hands me one, sitting cross-legged beside me. The first slurp burns my mouth.

"Patience," says Tenzin, gesturing to Kailash, as if I must slow my sipping, not for him but for *Kang Rinpoche*, this exhalation of mystery that has just begun to reveal its secrets. We sit in silence and sip tea, a pair of witnesses.

Today is meant for acclimatization before walking over the high-elevation pass tomorrow. Adjacent to Camp One is Dirapuk Monastery, the most important structure built at the base of Kailash. Dirapuk was established after the sage Gotsampa, first to encircle the mountain, stopped at its rock alcove for rest and prayer. The chamber would remain undisturbed for thousands of years, until eventually becoming a known refuge for ascetics.

As morning turns to day, the monastery door swings open and Pierre enters. Something in his jacket pocket bulges. He shifts through the chamber illuminated by hundreds of butter candles. The door shuts. A current in the room shifts. Flames stand erect. Pierre's movements turn sharp and calculated. Nothing distracts him, neither the mural paintings peeling from the walls nor the Tibetan monk-in-training at the entrance collecting Chinese yuan to continue the eroded legacy of his people. Pierre peers into a crack in the rock as light from butter flames exposes an intensity. He pulls a black 35mm film container from his pocket and pops the top to take a pinch of something clay-like from it before rolling a blueberry-sized piece between thumb and forefinger. After kneading the pellet, Pierre squats and murmurs with shut eyes. He brings the putty to his chest, delivers a bow, then pushes it tenderly into the crack with his finger, tender as if rejoining a hummingbird's femur. Pierre's head droops low enough for vertebrae to ripple through the back of his oversized hockey jersey. A moment or two later, the door creaks open and someone else enters the cave. Pierre quickly pockets his secret, prostrates three times, and exits the chamber.

• • •

IT ISN'T UNTIL THE THIRD AND MOST CONSEQUENTIAL DAY of the *kora*—up and over 18,500-foot Dolma La Pass—that the route finally begins to feel circular. I look ahead and see a Chinese tourist puttering up the path like an expired tractor. At this elevation, nothing much lives but the bucking prayer flags that carpet the pass. No power lines in the bardo. The wind cranks turbines and nothing surrounds the path but chalk-colored stone. Trailing the Chinese man is a Tibetan porter hunched under the weight of his client's gear. In addition to the sixty-five-pound pack, he holds an oxygen tank in the crook of his arm, a tan cylinder that looks like a missile. Plastic tubes connect the tank to a mask affixed to the face of the Chinese man, who sits hyperventilating by the side of the trail with his head between his legs. The porter stops. He doesn't complain, but he doesn't comfort his client, either. Instead, the man enjoys the break, rests the tank on his thigh, and reviews the pass ahead. Eventually, the tourist signals onward and the two stagger forward. Four steps. *Break.* Two steps. *Break.* One step. *Break.* The two remain connected, an umbilical adjoining of oxygen, keeping them both entangled, both alive.

In Robert Macfarlane's book *The Old Ways*, the author travels to China's Sichuan province to circumambulate its highest mountain, Minya Konka. He describes the crush of elevation while slogging over one of the mountain's high passes as some "medieval pain-helmet of pig-iron jammed down over the head." This feels accurate now, as the 18,500-foot pass overwhelms my vision and slows everything to a standstill. Hands on thighs, all I can do is concentrate on the next step. For Tibetans, reaching this crossing marks a moment of awakening, a kinesthetic passage through a bardo phase, after death but before rebirth, as if the pilgrim were surrendering her mortal fate and the backside descent pointed toward new life.

Bardo or no bardo, I feel like I am dying. Breath short and sticky, I've lost half my vision. Earlier, I'd caught Pierre kneeling by a boulder with something in his hand—more of that strange clay. I felt compelled to press on. Everything throbs as we crest the pass alongside dozens of others. Shared streams of intentionality. Detached discomfort. Bodies are often left on this pass to die, mainly Indian elders coming unprepared for the effort and falling dead in the attempt. No bodies this time, just three blue-black ponds reflecting an amphitheater of granite, liquid portals to the mountain's interior. This place is made for passage, not lingering. I put my head down, choose a line, and shuffle along, descending toward oxygen and life.

After a blur of downhill, an electrical storm unleashes its wrath on unprepared pilgrims. Flash. Deepening roar. Another flash. A tumble of rockslide in the distance. When

I arrive to camp, strong winds lean our cluster of yellow tents like a dozen fried eggs in a tilting pan. The crew had struck camp beside a river now bloated in its rush toward 750 million downstream. Headwaters. I arrive before dark and click on my headlamp to find a tent leaking at the seams. Backpack? Wet. Sleeping bag? Wet. Camera? Damn, wet. Lightning strikes close enough that I can feel it surge through the fillings in my teeth. Yvan, Nym, and Macy are still out there. I jump out of my tent, look for headlamps up the pass. Seeing none, I begin digging a circle around the tent's perimeter with a wedge of petrified yak dung, around and around as lightning cracks and thunder booms off Kailash's flank. I retreat into my tent, cowed by the elements.

Another hour passes before the others arrive. Yvan, the Thai filmmaker, collapses in his tent, nearly hypothermic, while Maddy, the American physician, provides supplemental oxygen. Nym films everything. I help ease their arrival and then run into Macy, the children's yoga instructor. She appears sopping wet and bite-sized in this landscape; I fear she might blow away. Through my headlamp I see her left eye is swollen and rimmed in what looks like tartar sauce, a white-green pus. She asks me to pry out a contact lens that had lodged into the back of her infected eye and hands me soft-tipped calipers along with a desperate smile. I fish it out under the mess tent while clouds stack on top of each other, booming heavy.

• • •

ON THE FOURTH AND FINAL LEG OF THE CIRCUIT, A FLAT, ten-mile return to Darchen, the sky clears and the river next to our camp babbles as if it had never raged at all. Macy's eye swelled shut overnight. Yvan responded well to the oxygen, but remains short of breath. Every ounce of our gear is soaked, and others disperse to take stock of gear and hang things in the warming sun. Baker stands in the mess tent with Tenzin and the porters, hands on his hips to debrief the night and make plans for the days ahead. Tenzin looks sober. No cigarette. No jokes. After breaking camp, the group continues on, following a path exposed and dry, not nearly as dramatic as the Lha Chu side. Green tufts of grass dot the sides of the trail and the air is unmoving and warm, like a high desert pause. Kailash already feels behind us, but never far.

I choose to walk alone. If there had indeed been a bardo crossing last night, it is far too early to say. The trash. The security detail. Pierre's daughter. The Chinese tourist. This group of spiritual tourists I've joined, here with our fluorescent tents and our prepared meals and our cute private bathroom tent. As each step closes in on completing the circuit, I find myself unsettled about being here, about pushing my way into such far-flung places just because I can. Why must I feel the need to always be moving at such voracious pace, always traveling to the edges and so radically far from home and, too often, far from myself? What exactly is it I've come to find?

Lost in thought, I nearly collide with a Bon pilgrim who is walking straight toward me at an aggressive clip. The Indigenous Bon are considered original practitioners of Tibet's folk religion, animistic doctrines performed by its earliest priests, which eventually incorporated ritual walking circles. The religion was established in western Tibet's Zhang Zhung kingdom several centuries before Buddhism arrived in the eighth century, where many Bon communities were absorbed into Buddhist enclaves over time—only 10 percent of Tibetans identify as Bon. Now, whenever a Bon pilgrim walks around Kailash, they travel counterclockwise, a subtle protest.

For Bonpo, the mountain was said to be the arrival site for Bon's founding father, Tonpa Shenrab. A feud broke out between Bon leader Naro Bonchung and the Buddhist *siddha* poet Milarepa. It was Milarepa who would claim victory and crown Kailash as Buddhist, its deity Chakrasamvara, the mountain's sole tenant. To complicate matters, Hindus place Shiva and Parvati at the summit, its northwestern slopes their private staircase home. Different histories, similar consensus: Kailash's summit is crowded, but only by gods.

As the Bon pilgrim disappears behind me, it's clear that they aren't the only ones who practice circumambulation counterclockwise. For the world's 1.6 billion Muslims, *tawaf*—Arabic for "circling"—marks the annual visit to Mecca for Hajj, a fifth pillar of Islam following declarations of faith, ritual prayer, alms, and fasting (Ramadan). The Hajj erupts over several days, the most highly attended circumambulation on the planet, counterclockwise, one that predates Muhammad, who was born in Mecca around 570 BCE. Before his birth, the story goes that the prophet Abraham and his family arrived to the area, in modern-day Saudi Arabia, where he and his son Ishmael built a version of today's Kaaba, the cubed structure you see resting at the heart of Mecca. Adam was the original architect, and Abraham and Ishmael had been restoring it after years of disrepair. With materials collected from five nearby mountains, Abraham placed at its core a black stone from heaven. Others say the stone was scrap material from Adam's original construction. After finishing the Kaaba, Abraham and Ishmael walked around it seven times counterclockwise to establish the inaugural *tawaf*. Mohammed would arrive later to encourage the pilgrimage, but it wasn't until his last year of life, in 632 BCE, that he first performed the walk:

> Behold, we gave to Abraham the site of the House; do not associate anything with Me (in worship!); and sanctify My House for those who circumambulate, or those who take their stand there (qa'mum), who bow or prostrate themselves there.

Now, when Muslims stop for calls to prayer each day—a quarter of the human population—they face in the direction of the Kaaba, the Black Stone, a spiritual source of gravity. For one week every October, several million Muslims from 188 countries arrive to the Hajj and overwhelm the region's capacity to house, feed, and tend to medical and safety needs. Hotels overbooked. Food and water trucked in. Forty-five thousand tents erected. Seven hundred fifty thousand sheep sacrificed. Five thousand surveillance cameras. Eighteen thousand police officers. Watch a video of the Hajj and it's unclear if you're witnessing a religious experience or a time-lapse swirl of the Milky Way.

The Bon pilgrim fires past me, embodying the many layers of occupation I'd found smashed up here at the base of Kailash. Bon. Hindus. Tibetan Buddhists. Chinese. And now, my North American arrival. As hundreds of thousands of exiled Tibetans are unable to travel back to their birthplace, I'm able to buy my way into witnessing a remote mountain on the edge of the Earth. There is imperial blood on my feet stamping all over this landscape, an imprint of outsiders searching for some curated sublime because perhaps we lost a certain quality of belonging in our own heart. Are we actually trading the *ego*centric for a more *eco*centric view, as Baker suggested, or is this all some charade to serve some private vacancy?

After several miles, Darchen comes back into view. We're scattered along the trail, and I notice that most are walking alone. The group returns to town and celebrates with a hot meal, but morale quickly sours as we're forced to stay another night in the cinder block barracks. "We want a hot shower," some protest. "Bathrooms, not blood-splattered holes." "Food, not yak-everything." Sauvignon and Scallops refuse to stay another night at the guesthouse and demand a Land Rover back to Lhasa. Maddy joins them, fed up with the lack of organization. Within two hours, three people and two guides leave, and the group reduces to twelve. Another storm envelops Kailash.

FOUR | *Bardo*

"Vite Monkey!" Uli's German accent cuts through the van as she ratchets open the window to take a photo. Kailash now in the rearview mirror, we have become a convoy of two vehicles returning to Lake Manasarovar after a spur west to the Guge Kingdom in Tholing, bordering Kashmir. This lake will be the last stop before Lhasa and a long return home.

"You mean wild donkey?" Tenzin says, correcting her and laughing hard enough for the hand-rolled cigarette wedged atop his ear to fall to the van floor. Tenzin swivels his flat-brimmed cap backward to pick it up, exposing an American flag printed on its underside. His baby-blue V-neck droops low, and bleached hair sticks out from beneath the hat. The twenty-five-year-old Tibetan exudes confidence and a two-second attention span while across his cheek runs a scar that resembles the thousand-foot avalanche chute on Kailash.

Indeed, a wild donkey stands alert in the plains a hundred yards from the highway. Her cream-white underbelly fades into coffee-hued flanks ribbed and muscular, to meet paintbrush bristles finning along the spine. These native kiang prefer sweeping grasslands and don't venture below nine thousand feet. Viewed from the side, their body seems to map the very topography of this plateau—underbelly of

Himalayan peak hemmed in by glacier rounding north to a barrel-bodied expanse of earth browns and slate.

The kiang canters away with a pace conjuring stories of the *lung-gom-pa,* Tibetan wind runners. These elusive monks are fabled to cover two hundred miles on foot in a single day by setting their gaze on something in the distance, like a mountaintop. To train, the *lung-gom-pa* would dig holes in the ground the depth of their bodies and sit long in meditation before bounding with all their might from the pit. This trained the wind runners for explosive movement, a lightness of body readying them for near-limitless foot travel across high-elevation grasslands—perhaps the original ultrarunners.

Only a few recorded sightings exist of the *lung-gom-pa,* one of the earliest being from Alexandra David-Néel, a German anarchist opera singer famous for traveling through Tibet in the 1920s disguised as a begging yak herder. One striking image of David-Néel depicts her as a stern foreigner with a rosary hung around her neck made from 108 different human bones, while a trumpet carved from a femur dangles from her hip. David-Néel's travels were unprecedented for European women at the time. In 1924, when the first British expeditions were charting their initial ascent of Kailash, she wrote while traveling through northern Tibet: "I noticed... a moving black spot which my field-glasses showed to be a man." As her caravan got closer to the traveler, it appeared to be an entranced monk who "seemed as if carried on wings."

Since the Chinese occupation in 1950, few Tibetans practice this form of wind running anymore. Like *kora,* such traditions chafe against a modernizing China and were restricted during the Cultural Revolution, a prohibition that is suggestive of a growing ecocultural hush sweeping the plateau.

Pre-occupation, Tibet rumbled with wildlife. Bar-headed geese were known to fly level to the summit of Mount Everest at 29,500 feet, considered the most extreme migration on the planet. The Fourteenth Dalai Lama's earliest childhood recollections from the 1930s—before escaping to exile in India—included "immense herds of kiang and *drong* (wild yaks) freely roaming the plains." Chinese settlement has since decimated large populations of raptors, foxes, wolves, and bears. Sixty percent of Tibet is considered grassland, traditional grazing habitat for a number of species, like kiang, but with a rapidly warming climate and increased oil, gas, and mining development here, nonhuman communities are forced to the margins.

Chinese authorities counter this alarming trend with appeals to the benefits of modern medicine, infrastructural support, and greenwashing rhetoric, transforming Tibet into a tapestry of national reserves, a recreational Edenic playground that serves as a backdrop for human activity. Human rights activists see these plans as "paper parks," campaigns to gain buy-in in order to secure future extraction and hydroelectric investments. In *To a Mountain in Tibet*, British writer Colin Thubron journeyed to circumambulate Kailash following the death of his mother. In his well of grief, he writes of the unspoken Tibetan sentiment: "Somewhere in these wilds they may whisper to the fierce mountain gods to bring back the Dalai Lama to Lhasa, and drive the Chinese out."

I watch as this solitary animal, steady as the *lung-gom-pa*, bolts across the plains in the distance. The week I arrived in Lhasa, two men made headlines for chasing down and hitting a kiang with their sport utility van. One of the men, Chen Haisheng, a Chinese railway tycoon—allegedly the only man in Lhasa to own a Ferrari—walked from his SUV after ramming the animal and hacked the injured kiang with a machete, gutting it and taking it home as a trophy. The slaughter was noted only because he posted images online, in blue jeans and Ray-Bans, grinning with endangered animal blood up to his elbows.

...

TONIGHT'S CAMP SETS ALONG THE NORTHWESTERN SHORE of Lake Manasarovar, one of the highest freshwater bodies on the planet, before we make a thousand-mile drive east to Lhasa. To the north, Kailash wrestles with thunderheads. To the south, Gurla Mandhata rises to 25,243 feet, the highest peak in the Nalakankar Himal. And to the west, a second, sickle-shaped lake, Rakshas Tal, connects to Manasarovar by a short channel, the Ganga Chu. From satellites, these two lakes appear as lungs offering breath to Kailash, ovarian bodies unionized with Kailash's phallic uplift. In *Circling the Sacred Mountain*, Buddhist academic Robert Thurman and his group stopped here at the lakeshore, where he recalls rumors of the Chinese "wanting to drain Lake Manasarovar for the gold ... The Tibetans believe the gold to be excrement of dragons, the implication being that you mustn't mess with dragons."

Tashi and I walk along the lakefront after a dinner of lentils as the sky streaks in colors of faraway. He seems right at home, moving at a professional ease with his electric-blue ball cap, leather cut-off gloves, and an up-collared windbreaker embroidered with his company's name.

"I hope this will all get better," Tashi says. "Everything's changing so quickly in China. I don't think their leaders mean to do something corrupt like this; it's more the small people working for the government who do bad things. But we younger people? We are stronger now to protect our culture, to protect our language. I mean, there's even Tibetan script for iPhones now. That's good, right?"

I recall reading about widespread extraction of rare earth metals in Tibet to produce the beloved devices that connect us, that translate our words, that bring Tashi and me together for this very exchange, ecological taxation in the form of extraction of the copper, gold, lithium, and nickel held by this plateau. "The way I see it," he adds, "if no language exists, we don't exist."

I wonder how Tashi thinks of preserving the practice of *kora* for future generations, much like preserving a language. "Are practices like *kora* even still relevant for young Tibetans anymore?" I ask. "Would you consider *kora* to be its own sort of language?"

"You make of *kora* what you will," Tashi responds. "Look, we have so many holy mountains here. We also have many mines. I find it curious that the people who mine here only seem to find their fortunes in holy mountains. Tibetans believe that if you mine a holy mountain, you'll have an unlucky life. I agree. The main reason why my people started to perform *kora* around these mountains in the first place was to protect them!" Tashi balls his fists, careful not to share too much frustration, almost as if our van's Chinese-issued speed governor was somehow monitoring his innermost truth; this could prove dangerous for a young Tibetan's career. As the evening purples and wind picks up, we follow the lakeshore and land in silence until our yellow tents come back into view.

• • •

STORIES OF UNEXPLAINABLE PHENOMENA SURROUND Lake Manasarovar, which is what grabs my attention after light pulses from the water's edge in the middle of the night to meet my tent. Finding my glasses, I peer into the strobe and see that it is not some dragon encounter or floating deity, but rather Pierre blinking his flashlight at me. I curse under my breath, put on a puffy, and walk toward the light. Before going to bed, I had fallen nauseous again from the high elevation, when Pierre asked for a favor.

"Hey, kid, can you do something for me?" For three weeks we shared a van and guest rooms, and I could no longer take his antics. We all felt the same way. Pierre constantly lectured Baker, Tenzin, and Tashi about Tibetan history, about Kailash, about Guru Rinpoche. "*Gooo-Rooo*," he would say with rotten apricot breath. No one spoke with him at length anymore except for me.

"Can you wake me up at two in the morning?" he asked.

"No way," I replied. "You've got an alarm clock."

"Come on, mine just ran out of batteries and I need to wake up. This lake, it's magic, man. Something else. Join me! We'll sit and watch for serpents and crazy fucking shit. Greatest show on Earth." His eyes looked desperate this time. His typical leaping and bounding and know-it-all attitude had shifted into a plea for help.

"Okay, Pierre, I'll wake you up," I said. "I'll join you, but only for a few minutes."

Wind shudders across the lake's surface to scatter its reflection of stars in every direction.

"Sorry, man." he says. "Couldn't sleep. Just too exciting."

I am about to scold Pierre for waking me up when something darts across the lake's surface. A silver pyramid begins to speed toward us in ripples, galloping and vaulting across the water like *kiang*, like *lung-gom-pa*, like *dakinis*. The light draws closer to expose two camp chairs Pierre set up.

Moonrise.

The encroaching orb peeks above the mountains to the east and radiates across the water at a freight train's pace. The balance of this moment, this unexplainable land where a teetering moon above and a burrowing sun below hold two lakes and two mountains in perfect balance, death of the sun inviting this rise of the moon, seems too vast to know fully. This moment needs nothing. The display removes me from Pierre, who squats now by the lake with something in his hand. It's the film canister. That purple clay. Pierre is rolling its contents into a small ball again, and I've had enough guessing. I need to know. As I approach, the lake whirlpools in moonlight.

"It's for my daughter," Pierre says, anticipating my question. "It *is* my daughter."

No sound.

No movement.

Only moon.

"My daughter. Rebecca. She was fifteen when she died. Cardiac arrythmia. Malfunction of the heart's electrical grid. Came out of nowhere, less than a year after her diagnosis. Gone. Fucking gone. Such a smart, talented girl. Too young, too soon." He stops for a breath. Looks at the lake. "Purple was her favorite color, so I mixed the last of her ashes into this Play-Doh and have been returning tiny bits of her to these sites—Jokhang, Dirapuk, Dolma La, Manasarovar—the most powerful places I know."

The moon is now a bowl of cream, and all I can see is Pierre's drooping face as it stills at the water's edge. I had single-mindedly wished to travel to Kailash in order to experience an unconquered mountain at close range, but perhaps this, too, is part of the *kora*, part of what I'd been summoned to walk around, to slow down enough to find compassion for what was in front of me all along: a despondent father with the ashes of his daughter in a pocket. Though I carry an aversion for Westerners assuming that scattering ashes on occupied lands is permissible, something in me waivers as Pierre faces the dark with his daughter in hand. I place my hand on his shoulder as it slouches in surrender. He finishes kneading the clay, takes a breath, and tosses it underhand into the lake.

 I imagine his daughter, a pea-sized ball of ash, seesawing to the bottom of the lake, traceable only by a string of silver air bubbles among Mani stones and millions of prayers. Pierre had begun making peace with his loss, and now his suffering spills over to me. He rests his hand on my shoulder and we embrace, both of us smeared in tears as we stumble back to the camp chairs. Slumping into the seat, I pull my sleeping bag close and watch as the lake's surface ripples out into larger rings, before eventually stilling to glass.

FIVE | *Return*

AFTER RETURNING TO LHASA, TONIGHT MARKS THE FINAL evening before flights home. Baker had organized a farewell dinner before melting back to his hidden *beyuls*. I wonder if the Nepali police will ever catch him, or where his future underworld explorations will take him next. The rest of the group shares hugs and goodbyes and now scatters to prepare for a long return. Macy's tartar-sauce eye is healed. Rodney has several new Himalayan recipe ideas for his dehydrated backpacking food company. Yvan and Nym catch the first taxi they can for some last-minute B-roll. And Tashi and Tenzin wait around until the end, forcing smiles through it all.

I find myself standing again with Pierre at the entrance of the Jokhang in Lhasa—full circle—staring at an oversized prayer wheel fixed above the monastery. It does not spin. *Mani khorlo*, they're called in Tibetan. *Mani*—jewel, *khorlo*—circle, or cycle. An encyclical of jeweled prayer. These wheels are used in Tibet and around the world for ritual, spun clockwise like *kora* to symbolize the ever-spinning, ever-revolving samsara and wheeling cosmos. Lining monasteries and temples, *mani khorlos* are often covered in sheet metal and embossed with Sanskrit prayer, wheels skewered upright while passing devotees spin the barrels clockwise with their fingertips. For lubrication, monks will pour warm rapeseed oil down the shaft, which pools at its base. It can sometimes look like blood.

But this prayer wheel looks different. There is no oil, nor any blood. Its decorative trim, however, is bloodred. Over three feet tall, the Sanskrit-inscribed cylinder is bolted to a storefront wall next to the Jokhang, too high for anyone to spin. Much like the power lines and security scarecrows, this *mani khorlo* is stationary. I peer up at the oversized prayer. It stares back and it does not spin because, upon closer review, inside the bowels of this wheel rests not divine emptiness or germinating prayer, nor any centrifugal offerings of merit or cosmic orientation. No, inside this prayer wheel hums a camera, cold metal gathering footage of the streets and this circuit providing orientation for so many, a machine that blinks its red eye every fifteen seconds, a feature hardly noticeable against the backdrop of its bloodred trim. Only when I slow down and come closer can I see it.

Three Tibetan elder women pass through the military checkpoint before entering the palace grounds to start their evening revolutions. Satchels and handheld prayer wheels slide through the X-ray machine. The soldiers hardly move. An officer holds a semiautomatic in one arm and a "butterfly catcher" in the other, a metal hoop affixed to a pole. The tool reminds me of the clothes hanger hoops I used to make with my father growing up, untwisting the wire and shaping it into a large ring, then dipping them in soapy water to wave in the sky, making green-purple iridescent bubbles, pluming off like a suspended oil spill.

These "butterfly catchers" are for snatching self-immolators—those who light themselves on fire in protest of Chinese occupation—from a safe distance. Of the one hundred and fifty such *bodhisattva-phoenixes* in Tibet and China who have made an appearance since 2009, two were on the square of concrete where I stand. One was reduced to bone and ash; the other was caught midburn, the worst phase. First stop, hospital. Second stop, jail. Officials erased the horror from the streets in fifteen minutes. The final three requests left by a recent young self-immolator to his family haunt me still:

Be united.
Study Tibetan culture.
On fire I burn.

The streets of Barkhor glisten from an afternoon rain. From my left pocket, I smell the sandalwood mala beads Tenzin gifted me on the bus earlier in the day. The offering surprised me, Tenzin with his beautiful acne, his American flag flat-brim, the rage burning but concealed behind his eyes, shoving prayer beads into my hand and holding them there for a full minute before turning his eyes back to the road. I returned the favor, taking his hand and opening it to offer my knife. Tenzin grinned as I showed him how to disengage the safety, and he flipped it open right there in the swerving van. He never postured like I did about being unworthy to receive the gift. He never said thank you, and I didn't need it.

The elders begin their evening laps. Mantra gurgles from their chapped mouths as the alley falls silent. Silent like the grasslands. Silent like Kailash at dawn. Silent like a purple ball of bone-ash at the bottom of a lake. Silent like the eye of a storm. The walkers bob swiftly like buoys, prayer beads dangling from their left hands, each bead rubbed and then passed along in endless motion. In their right hands, a handheld *mani khorlo* spins with great force. One woman wears white sneakers that squeak with every step, as a Tibetan boy wearing a black Misfits shirt and a pot-leaf ball cap splits between them in a jog, modernity cutting through an Indigenous weave of multicolored aprons, a modern-day *lung-gom-pa*.

Pierre and I fall in behind them as evening falls and the sage pyres burn to ash. I try to attend each footstep, each step its own summit, but instead my mind scatters like buckshot. Pierre walks ahead and melts into the evening. I never see him again.

I walk around the Jokhang, thirteen revolutions, one hundred and eight minutes exactly. At the beginning of this journey, I had become so entranced by *kora*'s counterpoint to conquering summits, a kinesthetic gesture of restraint seeded first around Boudhanath, then running around volcanoes in the Pacific Northwest, and now here. I assumed that this *kora* would somehow gift me a breadcrumb, that if only I continued to follow this way around, I might realize some grand truth about ego and power and Self. But now I'm not so sure.

For the past decade, I had been seeking a shape to guide me on how to be in right relationship with a world and a culture moving at breakneck speed, how to remain centered in a world that had lost its center, but what I confronted here proved far more complicated. I broke into an occupied territory, a landscape straddling modern and ancient myths, a country on indefinite house arrest. Any easy truth found around this mountain had become far more abstruse. Pierre and his dead daughter. Spiritual tourism. The historical layer cake of loss and grief and rage. What or whom am I encircling? Where exactly is gravity? And what distinguishes a power line from a prayer flag, a mountain from a self, a storm from a song?

ROUND TWO | *Tamalpais*

"Life itself is revolutionary, because it constantly strives to surpass itself."

—Thomas Merton

THE SECOND ROUND REVEALED ITSELF A YEAR AFTER returning from Mount Kailash, this time far closer to home. Having traveled more than seven thousand miles to Tibet's western edge with an expectation that I would gain clear insight into how this five-thousand-year-old tradition of walking in circles might induce a sense of belonging for our times, what I found was something more interesting and complicated, more mud than lotus, more bramble than meadow. The prodigal son fable of Ganesh and Kartikeya haunted me still, two brothers tasked with racing three times around the world, where the first to return would receive the luscious mango of wisdom. Ganesh won not by peacocking afield, but rather by staying home and stomping his elephant feet three laps around his parents.

 I had taken the route of Kartikeya, traveling as far afield as I could for that mango, first with the around-the-world trip, then with ultrarunning, and then the walk around Kailash. But this striving mindset only perpetuated a sense of not-enoughness. It felt as if these early trips were more circum*navigation* than circum*ambulation*. Ferdinand Magellan circumnavigated. In Jules Verne's *Around the World in Eighty Days,* Phileas Fogg circumnavigated. Herman Melville's Ahab in *Moby Dick* circumnavigated: "There is much in that sound to inspire proud feelings; but whereto does all that circumnavigation conduct? Only through numberless perils to the very point whence we started, where those that we left behind secure, were all the time before us."

Kailash was different. Kailash introduced me to the essence of circumambulation. Kailash left me curious about finding more circuitous prayer routes closer to home. That's when I found it one day in *Mountains and Rivers Without End* (1996), a book of poetry by Gary Snyder. It was a mango, unlocked not through planetary galivanting, but by staying close to the source. The next round wrapped around a mountain far less dramatic, but no less magical: Mount Tamalpais, an hour north of San Francisco and sixty miles from where I was born in Redwood City, California. Snyder lived upon its slopes and wrote about the mountain in a way that would turn his poetry into a treasure map, a map without an X to mark the spot. Because Snyder understood, like Ganesh, that the circuits around the local, the Self, the Mother—spoke directly to the circumambulator's central mantra: *There's nowhere else to go.*

•••

THE FIRST TIME GARY SNYDER WITNESSED RITUAL WALKING in circles was in the 1950s, while studying in Japan. Drawn to Eastern languages, the young poet from the Pacific Northwest toggled between school—Reed College, Indiana University, UC Berkeley—and work as a lumberjack, trail crewman, and fire lookout ranger. Arriving to Kyoto in 1956, Snyder would spend the next decade in Japan, and it was upon the slopes of Mount Hiei where he learned of the *yamabushi* mountain ascetics. One method they used for prayer included walking around mountains and temples, including Kaihōgyō, a grueling thousand-day circuit.

These devotional routes were etched onto Snyder's imagination when, in the winter of 1962, he and his first wife, Joanne Kyger, left Kyoto to travel for several months through Sri Lanka and India, a trip documented in Snyder's *Passage Through India* (1972) and Kyger's *The Japan and India Journals* (1981). The two departed by steamer to Hong Kong, lying on the ship's deck at night smoking handrolls and identifying southern stars. They tacked through Vietnam and Singapore, where Snyder would pick up dysentery, and then went on to Colombo and Kandy in Ceylon, present-day Sri Lanka. The two traveled light. "They know our sort of tourist (rucksack) and know we don't bring much in dollar," wrote Snyder after being eyed by a customs agent. In Kandy, they straddled elephants and studied Hindu and Buddhist architecture, including Dalada Maligawa, the Temple of the Tooth, where an incisor from the Buddha was said to be encased in its inner sanctum.

Drifting north into Anuradhapura, the former capital of Sri Lanka, Snyder wrote his first entry about circular pilgrimage: "Next to the site is a large pond, fringed with lovely trees. A few pious Buddhists circumambulating the stupas." From Pondicherry, a former French station, their journey continued to Tiruvannamalai, where the two joined in *pradakshina* around the base of the Shaivite mountain, Arunachala. Their first encounter with Tibetan *kora* came later, when they reached Bodh Gaya in India's northeastern Bihar, where the Buddha was said to have attained enlightenment. Here they found Tibetans walking "day and night, whirling their prayer wheel" around the Mahabodhi temple and the Bodhi tree. Snyder witnessed *kora* in Kathmandu, too, around the Boudhanath temple where my first encounter took place in 2006. The shape was beginning to shape him.

Returning to Madhya Pradesh, India, the two visited the Khajuraho temple built in the eleventh and twelfth centuries during the peak of Tantric Hinduism, and they'd spend hours running their fingers across engravings of tangled humans having carnal sex in every possible contortion. Snyder compared this temple to Kailash. In Delhi, they connected with Allen Ginsberg and his partner, Peter Orlovsky. Together the foursome visited the German-born poet, Sri Lama Govinda, who had left Europe in the 1930s to become a monk in Sri Lanka and ended up in Kasar Devi. In his book, *The Way of the White Clouds* (1966), Govinda describes early encounters of *kora*, expressing a distaste for Western colonial approaches to landscape, and finding more authority in the sanctity of mountains than in the egocentricity of man:

> The personality of a mountain is more than merely a strange shape that makes it different from others... Personality consists in the power to influence others, and this power is due to consistency, harmony, and one-pointedness of character. If these qualities are present in an individual, in their highest perfection, then this individual is a fit leader of humanity, either as a ruler, a thinker, or a saint, and we recognize him as a vessel of divine power. If these qualities are present in a mountain, we recognize it as a vessel of cosmic power, and we call it a sacred mountain. The power of such a mountain is so great and yet so subtle that, without compulsion, people are drawn to it from near and far, as if by the force of some invisible magnet... This worshipful or religious attitude is not impressed by scientific facts, like figures of altitude, which are foremost in the mind of modern man. Nor

is it motivated by the urge to "conquer" the mountain. Instead of conquering it, the religious-minded man prefers to be conquered by the mountain.

The poets drifted farther into northwest Punjab and Dharamsala, where they holed up in opium dens to await an appointment with His Holiness the Fourteenth Dalai Lama, then only in his midtwenties. When they finally met, Snyder and the Dalai Lama discussed meditation techniques, while Ginsberg wanted his take on psychoactive drugs. After the meeting, the group took a train to Delhi and Bombay, then Snyder and Kyger cut south to catch a boat in Colombo to Saigon, Hong Kong, and back to Japan.

In 1965, Snyder returned to San Francisco and settled in Mill Valley, a then humble town at the foot of a still-humble mountain—Mount Tamalpais. By that time, he'd learned a great deal about Eastern languages and traditions, including circuitous pilgrimage, and wished one day to "see if we couldn't find a way to do that elsewhere." On October 22, 1965, he got his wish.

Joined by Ginsberg and the Zen poet Philip Whalen, the three sketched a fifteen-mile loop starting at Redwood Creek, Muir Woods National Monument, spiraling clockwise west and north up the coast, around the north side and up to Tamalpais's high point, East Peak, before returning to Redwood Creek. Posing a distinct contrast to Kailash, this route incorporated the peak as one of its twelve "stations." They spent all day following the path, and Snyder would later include a poem about the walk in *Mountains and Rivers Without End*, an epic composed over forty years—1956 to 1996—considered one of the greatest works of modern poetry. "The Circumambulation of

Mount Tamalpais" starts by walking with Snyder's clear vision: "Walking up and around the long ridge of Tamalpais, 'Bay Mountain,' circling and climbing—chanting—to show respect and to clarify the mind. Philip Whalen, Allen Ginsberg, and I learned this practice in Asia. So we opened a route around Tam. It takes a day."

STATION ONE | *Redwood Creek*

EIGHTEEN STRANGERS FORM A CRESCENT SHAPE, THEIR eyes closed and heads bowed at the edge of Redwood Creek, three miles upstream from Muir Woods. Some wear jeans and cotton; others, polypropylene and synthetics. Skies above smear in charcoal and whiff of blue gum eucalyptus and bay laurel as a crow threads the canopy. *Whoosh.* No one notices because the leader of the day, Oren Davis, hands out chanting sheets to welcome everyone, and he begins the recitations: *Mantra to Purify the Site* and *The Dharani of Removing Disasters, Heart Sutra.*

> OM RAKSHA RAKSHA HUM HUM HUM
> PHAT SVAHA

It's Sunday morning and day hikers mill about the parking lot, some looking up from their devices and paper-cup Americanos, curious about the noise. I tuck my voice behind the group, self-conscious about having organized this event and now, reciting a mantra in a language foreign to me. I take stock of my day's provisions:

> glass jar of spearmint tea,
> jack cheese and avocado on cracked wheat,
> small bag of Medjool dates,

chocolate bar, the darkest I could find,
coffee-stained paperback copy of Snyder's *Mountains and Rivers Without End*.

I'd dog-eared his poem, "The Circumambulation of Mount Tamalpais," because today these words would serve not only as reading material, but as a map. For the past several months I'd been retracing this poem step by step, word for word, in an attempt to organize a fifty-year anniversary of the first round of Tamalpais by Snyder, Ginsberg, and Whalen, starting and ending here at Redwood Creek.

Coho salmon the length of major league baseball bats used to belly up here to spawn, one of the last native strongholds in California, but these days the flow is so low a pair of feet wouldn't even be able to soak in its shallows—the state is experiencing its worst drought in 1,200 years. Follow Redwood Creek toward the Pacific Ocean and you'll reach Muir Woods, a grove of coast redwoods two hundred and fifty feet high and eight centuries old, saplings during the Crusades, clustered elders once known not by humans but by one-ton grizzly bears and condors with ten-foot wingspans. All of this clusters at the base of Tamalpais, a two-headed summit with 360-degree views reaching out across the Bay Area estuary to the south, lakes to the north, and the Pacific Ocean to the west.

The mountain is a product of subduction, east-west collision, the Farallon Plate tucking beneath a more pliable North American continent to lift its edge and create a headlands. Volcanic sediment accreted into what's known as the "Franciscan Assemblage," fissures and cracks that bedazzle this coastal edge with minerals like serpentine—California's state rock—and blueschist, a glittered mélange. Although twenty thousand vertical feet shorter than Mount Kailash, Tamalpais is twice as old. Tamalpais formed over 100 million years ago, its east face resembling more of a Fuji-like ramp, while the western-facing edges jumble and toss more anarchic. But what surrounds a mountain is never quite as revealing as what's beneath, for this collision created these hills, hills that carved valleys, and valleys that set creeks into motion—*mountains and rivers without end*—and at once we have a 2,571-foot beacon of convergence, an axle spun to the tune of a most peculiar human tradition.

STATION TWO | *Tree Out of Rock*

THIS IS THE ONLY RULE OF THE DAY: SILENCE UNTIL THE summit. The fifteen-mile route starts by heading west to the ocean, then traverses bluffs north along the coast before curling inland and around Tamalpais's remote north side to connect with a spur trail that leads to the summit, followed by a descent back to Muir Woods. The group crosses the creek to follow the historic Dipsea Trail, where, after two miles, we stop at a live oak hemmed in by small boulders, regrouping under ornamental lime-green lichen. This was where Snyder, Ginsberg, and Whalen established their second "station." I recall starting around Kailash and how it all felt so linear at first, and this feels no different.

In Marin artist Tom Killion's book, *Tamalpais Walking* (2009), he asked Snyder, a close friend, why he included the summit with the route, and his answer thudded with practicality. "I didn't really know the north side of the mountain very well," said Snyder. "And I didn't want to go down in the brush—it's hot down there. So I thought, why not go to the top? It's got that little trail that goes around it, just below the summit. So you could climb up to that, go around it and right up to the summit, and then come down: the *spiral* climb."

Snyder cited that *yamabushi* routes in Japan often represented less a clean orbit and more of a mandala shape, where the pilgrim "sees the whole landscape," which can sometimes include a visit to its inner core. "If you can include the valley bottom *and* the top in the same trip you really get them, well... this is not Mt. Kailash."

He was right; this was not Kailash. This was a whole new spin on the art of walking in circles, and in my case it felt far more personal. There were two reasons why I organized this walk. First, it was true that a desire to honor Gary Snyder had set me on this path. Tamalpais was his training ground for exploring a convergence of ecology, spirituality, and activism. The poet sought radical attention during a time of globalization and runaway materialism, a post–World War II era that left much of America in hot pursuit of safety, suburban conformity, and consumerism fed on cheap fuel. I was drawn to Snyder's bioregional literacy, his reverence and study of Indigenous ways of knowing, and for his interest in a place's interiority. What struck me the most about his Tamalpais walk was that it seemed to incorporate all these values into one simple shape, a narrative aesthetic I could follow in my body. The first poem in his forty-year epic collection is called "Endless Streams and Mountains," and it ends like this:

> Walking on walking,
>   under foot   earth turns.
> Streams and mountains never stay the same.

To Snyder, the Earth is always moving. Mountains shape watersheds that shape valleys that move in lockstep with one another, and we too shape this land with our feet and our movements and our thoughts, just as the land shapes us. Snyder seemed to suggest that the path followed becomes a centering force, a bellwether in a storm, that there may be no center because everything is center, echoing Joseph

Campbell: "... if you didn't realize that the center was also right there facing you in the other person. This is the mythological way of being an individual. You are the central mountain, and the central mountain is everywhere."

The second reason for organizing this walk has nothing to do with poetry, however. I am also here because of cancer. While researching Tamalpais, the name Laura Pettibone kept surfacing as the leader of the walk, and it was only after talking on the phone and meeting her several times that I learned of her metastatic tumor. I became invested in Laura's recovery and wished to see her complete this anniversary walk, a confidence boost as she trudged through rounds of chemotherapy. I also wondered if my fixation on this stranger's healing had become a proxy for something closer to home—the discovery of my own mother's emergent breast cancer.

Laura and my mother both found cancer cells colonizing their bodies at exactly the same time. By growing closer to Laura, I was beginning to unlock a certain willpower to tend to my mother's illness. A woman of profound honesty, Mom hardened and further isolated herself, which resulted in a wedge between us, a permafrost not soon to thaw. But her challenges were not her own—they never are. They stemmed from an early love for, and intense pressure to, become the best female tennis player in the world from her father, who was also her coach. Clarence Carter—everyone called him Nick, for whom I was named—was a formidable man in Northern California's tennis scene, legendary for his coaching prowess and also for carrying on extramarital affairs. This would foster irreconcilable mistrust from my mother, which would in turn contribute to ripping a marriage and our family apart.

Both Laura and my mother carried cancer in their bodies, but Laura carried something else. She carried this mountain. I wanted to see firsthand how this ritual I'd begun tracking around the world afforded Laura a similar tenor of consistency and purpose. Laura made it clear to me that Tamalpais provided her with an anchor, something to live for. My mother, on the other hand, had no beloved mountain to wrap herself around, no buoy for her private squalls. As I grew closer to Laura, I found myself beginning to show up for my mother in new ways, and, as the day of our Tamalpais round arrived, Laura had already begun to teach me not only how to walk around a mountain, but how to widen my circumference of compassion. Laura was teaching me how to become a mountain.

STATION THREE | *Ocean View*

ONE HOUR AFTER WALKING, THE TRAIL OPENS UP TO PANoramic views of the Pacific shimmering like buffed quartz, where, just beyond the surf, two plates meet. Onshore winds petrify curtains of cypress while a Steller's jay darts indigo across salted air, as I recount poet Lew Welch's "Ring of Bone" drifting along the mist:

> Praises Gentle Tamalpais
> Perfect in Wisdom and Beauty of the sweetest water
> and the soaring birds
> great seas at the feet of thy cliffs.

A hard-drinking friend of Snyder's, in 1971, Welch walked into the woods near Snyder's Sierra Foothills home, where it's thought that he shot himself. His body was never found.

The sixteen others mill about the viewpoint. Sarah, an animal rights activist with magenta hair and an origami crane tied to her pack next to a button that reads, "Tofu, The Other White Meat," squawks back at the jay. A graduate school friend and his father rummage through a bag of gorp. They'd grown up in Marin County and always heard legends of this walk. Next to them sit Meri and Mark Gonnerman, two Snyder scholars from San Jose. Mark has a ponytail, circular glasses, and a thick midsection covered by chinos, while Meri remains quiet, full of grace. I'd met Mark before the walk to learn about his book, *A Sense of the Whole*, the definitive guide to *Mountains and Rivers Without End*, considered Snyder's most complicated text. In 1997, Mark organized a conference at Stanford University, gathering poets, critics, and scholars from around the world to better understand the work. He compared this book to whitewater rafting: While most of Snyder's poetry is Class III rapids—capable of negotiating on your own—*Mountain and Rivers* is more like Class V. If you're going to make it out alive, you're going to need a guide.

Mike Scott and Victor Ichioka lean on a boulder. Ichioka is an aging Japan-born hippie from Oakland, wiry and joyous, despite his arthritic cadence. Scott is a retired UC Berkeley professor and coauthor of *Opening the Mountain*, the only book written solely about the history of this walk. Months earlier, the three of us met for coffee in Berkeley, to talk about the tradition that followed after the first 1965 circumambulation. The two described how the first "public" Tamalpais round occurred on February 10, 1967, where sixty people showed up, including a twenty-three-year-old kid named Matthew Davis. A black-and-white photo from this day shows Davis sitting beside Ginsberg as the unshaven Beat hunches over, shirtless and chanting. Davis wore a plain white t-shirt and thick-rimmed eyeglasses, more conventional than Ginsberg, but something sets him apart, as if he were listening to the cries of wolves. This moment would change his life forever.

Like Snyder, Matthew Davis lived at the foot of Tamalpais in Homestead Valley, where he would raise a family and live for most of his life. Working at a picture-framing shop, Davis developed a relationship with the mountain through volunteering, cycling, and walking its slopes daily. After 1967, Davis began to lead the "CircumTam" four times a year—every Sunday closest to the solstice and the equinox. He'd arrive at Redwood Creek to follow the same route clockwise with whoever showed up, sustaining this mountain ritual for the next four decades. In my correspondence with Snyder, he referred to Davis as the true *acharya* of Tamalpais, "the one who teaches by conduct," the one who lived one's principles of care and devotion. According to Snyder, no one knew or revered the mountain more than Davis. Unfortunately, in 2014, Davis was diagnosed with leukemia. Months later, he suffered a bicycle accident while heading to work, fracturing his hip. For the next year his health declined, and he was forced to stop leading the walks. On August 3, 2015, he passed away.

One of the last photos of Davis on the mountain was leading a chant with a signature red bandana around his neck and favorite Tamalpais Conservation Club shirt, the same one his son Oren wears today. In the photo he looks able-bodied, at ease in the moment, doing what he loved most, a humble caretaker, an acharya. He was home.

Station Three, Ocean View, marks one of Davis's favorite stops. Here, he would loft prayers across the Pacific to recognize Indigenous peoples around the world whose lands had been stolen, acknowledging that one need not look further than these headlands to find lands stolen from the Coast Miwok, Southern Pomo, and the Ohlone. I send prayers through my teeth to Tenzin and Mount Kailash. Laura Pettibone is the last to arrive, sweeping the route in back so no one gets left behind. A sun hat covers her shoulder-length hair the color of salmon. Laura's skin looks pale, wrinkled in parts and taut in others. At six feet tall, her trekking poles offer leverage for the early miles. To know Pettibone is to understand her infatuation with

Tamalpais. The fifty-two-year-old has completed the circuit more than anyone else alive; if she finished, today would be her ninetieth lap.

In 2010, Laura uncovered a seven-centimeter tumor—the diameter of a tennis ball—growing on the left side of her brain. Until that point, she had accompanied Davis for more than two decades. Four times a year, every year. "Tamalpais is the main thing in my life," Pettibone told me weeks before the walk. "I consider this my going to church. I'm not religious, but I carry out much of my spiritual life here on Tam. It's my community." She was first introduced to the route in 1988 while working for the Headlands Institute, a natural history center. The invitation came during a difficult time, after Laura had opened up about her homosexuality to her conservative family and was promptly exiled. It didn't help that her first dabbles in dating women crashed and burned. "At that point, I just needed to belong to something. To somewhere." That somewhere was Tamalpais.

Following Laura's cancer diagnosis, chemo forced her to stop attending these walks and devote all her focus to surviving. On good days she would load up a pack with heavy books and hike up and down the vertiginous avenues outside the Mission District apartment she shared with her wife, Anne. Laura returned to Tamalpais in 2012 for her first walk since treatment. She was back, but barely, as seizures and other complications slowed her recovery. Today, Laura is doubting herself because the previous week's chemo dose has stolen all her energy, but to complete ninety laps on the fiftieth anniversary of the tradition would be her greatest accomplishment, while also honoring Davis's death. After all, he had become a father figure to her.

STATION FOUR | *Lone Tree Spring*

WE RECITE THE FOUR CARDINAL DIRECTIONS UNDER THE shade of coast redwoods, following a chant sheet and led by Oren, who wears his father's shirt tucked into designer jeans. Oren moves fast, keen to finish early. He was only nine years old when he completed his first Tamalpais round. As a rebel teen, Oren would join his father whenever he wasn't busy or hungover.

"I'd drive back after partying all night and my dad would put out lunches," he told me. "All I had to do was stumble out of the car." He lives four hours north, in Mendocino County, with a sixteen-year-old son and a second wife, Willow, and his days are too busy as a landscape foreman to be coordinating these walks. He's concerned the tradition will die without his father.

The route follows the Old Mine Trail to Pan Toll Ranger Station, where our intimacy of silence sobers quickly when we are greeted by a busy parking lot gurgling with weekend recreationalists. A family of six clogs the path while the youngest, in slime-green sweatpants, wheels a Spiderman suitcase across the dirt and clips my toes. After refilling water, the group continues into being enveloped by smells of bay laurel and sounds of scuffing feet. Four miles in, a trail passes a cluster of madrones that spiral from the duff, making my face flush with their erotic burgundy torsos. The sensation evokes a certain cross-species sensuality, and I wonder, might the madrone feel similarly about me? When any such notion of entering into a landscape's emotional porosity arises, I always think of the Scottish writer Nan Shepherd's *The Living Mountain*, considered "the finest book ever written on nature and landscape in Britain." The masterwork offers exacting language of such radial knowing of place from the inside out.

Finished in 1945, Shepherd would shove the manuscript into a desk drawer after it was eschewed by a male-dominated publishing world. In the 1960s and 1970s, comparable authors of environmental literature were gaining interest—Chatwin, Baker, Matthiessen, Carson—and, in 1977, *The Living Mountain* was finally published. At that point, mountain literature had been largely written by men and focused on summits, while Shepherd's work challenged this approach. She knew the high country more than most, wandering her beloved Cairngorm Plateau in northeastern Scotland, "Britain's Arctic," where she found deep insights by going *into the mountain*, not single-mindedly *up*.

"I am on a plateau again," wrote Shepherd, "having gone round it like a dog in circles to see if it is a good place. I think it is, and I am to stay up here for a while."

In Robert Macfarlane's 2011 introduction to *The Living Mountain*, the author reinforces Shepherd's sentiment: "The pilgrim contents herself always with looking along and inwards to mystery, where the mountaineer longs to look down and outwards onto total knowledge." Fixate less on gaining a summit or destination, and we might experience the mountain in far more profound ways.

"Often the mountain gives itself most completely when I have no destination," writes Shepherd, "when I reach nowhere in particular, but have gone out merely to be with the mountain as one visits a friend with no intention but to be with him." *The Living Mountain* confirms Shepherd's attunement to the Cairngorms and, by extension, herself. "I now understand in some small measure why the Buddhist goes on pilgrimage to a mountain. The journey is itself part of the technique by which the god is sought. It is a journey into Being; for as I penetrate more deeply into the mountain's life, I penetrate also into my own. For an hour I am beyond desire. It is not ecstasy, that leap out of the self that makes man like a god. I am not out of myself, but in myself. I am. To know Being, this is the final grace accorded from the mountain."

STATION FIVE | *Bay Tree Glade*

AFTER FOUR HOURS, THE MILES START TO STACK IN MY legs. Overconfident as a long-distance runner used to covering this sort of mileage before breakfast, I underestimated the physical demands of the route. Today will likely require over ten hours afoot—assuming all goes as planned—as the pace is made slower by the twelve stations, the fifth of which we arrive at to find and read a passage next to a stand of oak: "To first peoples who ventured from Asia by land and sea. Some came here, becoming Miwoks, thriving thousands of years on these lands and waters."

Before extraction fever arrived with California's Gold Rush of the 1840s, and long before engineers built the Golden Gate Bridge in the 1930s, slathering it in "international orange" paint, the estuary of the San Francisco Bay Area flourished with an abundance of life. It is estimated that humans first arrived in the area some twenty-five thousand years ago, and it's thought to be the case that the Southern Pomo, Coast Miwok, and Muwekma Ohlone are descendants of Siberian tribes. Before the early Spanish made contact in the 1500s, half a million people lived in present-day California, several thousand in the Bay Area alone.

Native communities congregated around the bay for its agreeable climate and plentiful game, where the Coast Miwok diet depended largely on the sea—clams, oysters, fish, rockfish, salmon, steelhead—while deer, elk, and quail were abundant too. Perhaps the most important staple came from the oak, dependable acorns and buckeyes that are highly nutritious after they are leached and ground into meal. Laurels and berries offered sweetness, too, while a variety of plants and roots identified as medicine were used in nearly everything. Today, 850 Coast Miwok sites remain around Mount Tamalpais. The Huimen, a tribelet of the Coast Miwok, lived nearest the peak and were some of the first documented Indigenous communities to be drawn off the mountain and into the earliest Spanish missions of San Francisco.

The name *Tamalpais* is of Coast Miwok origin. *Tamal-* translates to "coastal" or "west," while *-pais* refers to "hill" or "mountain." Tamalpais—Coast Mountain. Coast Miwok never visited the summit, believing Coyote spirit lived there and it was better left alone. In the 1830s, San Francisco trader Jacob Leese traveled to the mountain to survey its peak. Chief Marin, the legendary Coast Miwok leader for whom Marin County is named, accompanied Leese but refused to summit. Leese ascended alone, marking the top with a cross made of oak branches. To the dismay of his people, Chief Marin was forced to join him. Described in *Chief Marin: Leader, Rebel, and Legend* (2007), one account says that the chief took off his red shirt before descending and hung it from Leese's oak cross, making it appear as if it bled.

The California Gold Rush would quickly transform the region into a major commercial hub. By 1860, the population swelled to more than fifty thousand settlers. (Today, more than seven million people reside in the Greater Bay Area.) Before the settlers arrived, some ten thousand grizzlies roamed this state. There were grizzly bears being shot and sold for steak in downtown San Francisco. Early accounts from Europeans included frequent bear encounters, and some were even caught swimming in the bay. One witnessed a grizzly being shot as it tried swimming up to a dinghy near Angel Island. Soldiers fired at the bear dozens of times, but the animal made its way to the boat, its claws marking the skiff's side, a harbinger of impending erasure, for the California grizzly is no more. The last official sighting was in 1924.

As our group walks north toward the mountain's interior, I imagine a one-ton cinnamon grizzly loping through San Francisco's Mission District, while a condor, also extirpated, floats above, two apparitions of an unrecognizable past. This bear tries to remember her sense pathways while the condor lifts along unseasonably warm thermals. The phantom ursine weaves through side alleys, pawing at dumpsters, attendant to each novel smell of grilled pupusas, garlic popping in a butter-cream sauce, clam chowder ladled into hollow sourdough, steam-pressed espresso. No longer able to navigate this estuary, she takes a right down a graffitied street, passing two entwined transient lovers and, in a gasp of smoke, escapes to another time, stitched to California's state flag as a consolation prize, a mascot of occupation.

Indigenous communities often interpret the Western fixation with summits as an extension of the settler-colonial enterprise. For many Native peoples, mountains are homes to gods or diabolical forces and are to be visited with honor and humility, not objectives to tackle or resources to collect, but gods to revere and, often, to be left alone.

In Australia, Uluru rests at the country's geographic center, a clump of sandstone rising three thousand vertical feet above sea level, most of it nestled underground. Uluru is an inselberg, an island mountain, held sacred by its aboriginal stewards for ten thousand years. It is said that Lungkata, Blue Tongue Lizard, once lived on this rock and was known to sometimes steal meat from Emu below. Emu wasn't thrilled by this, so one day Emu decided to build a bonfire and smoke out Blue Tongue Lizard from his cave. From ground level, you can look up to Uluru's flank and see a blue streak splashing down from a cave, a mark of forewarning: *Do not try and acquire what is not rightfully yours.*

Such myths offer the Indigenous Anangu an anchor in Uluru. For generations the rock was forbidden to climb except for their special Mala rites of passage, while the nearby Pitjantjatjara preferred to walk the six-mile path around its base. In 1788, Europeans arrived in Botany Bay, near Sydney, where 162,000 convicts were exiled to the continent in the decades that followed. Britain's newest exile colony would begin its systematic penetration of the continent, commencing decades of take-and-grab accumulation without a treaty. William Gosse was the first European to reach Uluru in 1873, but it was his right-hand man, Edwin Berry, who climbed the rock, to the dismay of the Anangu. The Australian government changed the name *Uluru*—"Great Pebble"—to "Ayers Rock," after Sir Henry Ayers, then chief secretary of South Australia.

Uluru quickly became targeted as a tourist destination, a must-visit site in the continent's Red Center. Visitors poured in during the 1950s, quickly desacralizing the landscape with hotels, petrol stations, roads, hiking tours, climbing tours, and offroad Segway tours. Tourists on their way to the top of Uluru would bypass the sign at its base stating: "Please don't climb. We invite you to walk around the base and discover a deeper understanding of this place." Despite the Anangu living here for over thirty thousand years, and despite multiple appeals to a tourism bureau not to permit any further climbing of Uluru, it wasn't until 1985 that their wishes were only partially recognized. The government agreed to return the area to its traditional stewards, with one stipulation: They must lease it back to the government for ninety-nine years. And climbing must still be permitted.

On October 26, 2019, after two hundred years of occupation, the Anangu finally won a battle to prohibit climbing on Uluru. Unlike what I'd found at the base of Kailash, occupying forces in Australia had attempted to dethrone the gods of Uluru by placing themselves at the top, a flagrant gesture of hegemony. Similarly, Mount Everest—*Sagarmatha* in Nepali; *Chomolungma* in Tibetan, "Goddess Mother of Mountains"—has been scaled more than five thousand times since its first 1953 ascent. The mountain is replete with controversy and angry gods, Indigenous aversion to overcommercializing and overpolluting despite its economic benefit to the region.

Beyond Everest and K2 stands Kanchenjunga, a Himalayan massif located in northeast India and tucked between Nepal and Bhutan that was once thought to be the highest point on the planet. (At 28,169 feet, Kanchenjunga is, in fact, the third-highest mountain.) Like Kailash and Tamalpais, local communities view Kanchenjunga as home to mountain gods. The Lepcha people live at Kanchenjunga's base and believe that the world's first couple, a sort of Himalayan Adam and Eve, was born from the snows of this summit, where a formidable goddess named Yuma Sammang lives. The Lepcha know also of a yeti-like creature named *Nee-gued*, who inhabits the mountain's base. In 1899, the first person to travel around the entire base of Kanchenjunga concluded that "it is guarded by the Demon of Inaccessibility ... for the express purpose of defense against human assault."

Enter Europeans. After a harrowing first attempt of Kanchenjunga's summit in 1955 by British mountaineers Joe Brown and George Band, the mountain was banned for climbing. But in the decades that followed, bribes cut this red tape. In all, two hundred parties have attempted to "conquer" Kanchenjunga, despite local protests. To this day, there is still no official summit record, for every expedition is now required to stop two hundred feet short of the summit, though it is hard to believe everyone complies. In 1994, the Bhutanese government prohibited climbing any mountain in the kingdom higher than 6,000 meters (19,685 feet) out of respect for local customs. Since 2003, mountaineering is entirely forbidden. Nearby Gangkhar Puensum, the highest unclimbed peak in the world at 7,570 meters (24,840 feet), remains untouched.

In the United States, Wyoming's Devil's Tower was established as the country's first national monument in 1906. Here, an 867-vertical-foot igneous intrusion reaches upward, revered for 10,000 years as a meeting place for Plains tribes—Cheyenne River Sioux, Lakota, Kiowa—a sacred land feature to be left alone. Enter Europeans. The first recorded ascent was in June 1893, by a pair of ranchers. Five thousand people now climb the tower annually, despite opposition by Native communities. Devil's Tower has become a world-class recreation destination and a popular rest stop along the all-American road trip. In 1977, an alien spaceship landed on its flattop summit in *Close Encounters of the Third Kind*.

"It would be like climbing a big old cross," said one Crow elder, which for me summons the image of Chief Marin's bleeding cross on Tamalpais. Each June, tribes hold ceremony at Devil's Tower, a name offensive to every Native community in the area. In 2015, leadership from a federation of tribes went to the US government to request changing the name, as it implies a form of sorcery or devil worship. The name "Devil's Tower" derives from a poor translation of what early settlers thought they heard when local chiefs had said, "Bad God's Tower." To the contrary, the Arapahoe call the tower "Bear's Tipi," the Kiowa "Aloft on a Rock," and the Lakota "Bear Lodge," as the area was replete with bears. Now, the most commonly accepted amalgam is *Mateo Tepee*. The tribal council suggested "Bear Lodge" to the Wyoming tourism bureau, to which they denied the request, saying it would be too much of a brand disruption.

In the American Southwest, Native tribes will sometimes encircle agricultural lands before planting seeds and growing crops, to bless soil into fertility. The Papago of southern Arizona walk around cornfields after planting four kernels in each hole. "Night after night the planter walks around his field 'singing up the corn.'" In *Black Elk Speaks* (1932), John Neihardt provided the first written English account of the Oglala Lakota medicine man's visions during the attempted extermination of Native peoples in North America. As a child, Black Elk recounted a Great Vision, the "whole hoop of the world," one of many "that made one circle, wide as daylight and as starlight, and in the center grew one mighty flowering tree to shelter all the children of one mother and one father. And I saw it was holy." Black Elk's sacred hoop drew a shape counter to that of Manifest Destiny, a unidirectional force that amassed land, people, and resources along its way. Following a *heyoka* ceremony, Black Elk examined this difference between the shape of Indigenous lifeways and the white man's hard-edged barracks:

> It is a bad way to live ... for there can be no power in a square ... You have noticed that everything an Indian does is in a circle, and that is because the Power of the

World always works in circles, and everything tries to be round. In the old days when we were a strong and happy people, all our power came to us from the sacred hoop of the nation, and so long as the hoop was unbroken, the people flourished... The sky is round, and I have heard that the Earth is round like a ball, and so are the stars. The wind, in its greatest power, whirls. Birds make their nest in circles, for theirs is the same religion as ours. The sun comes forth and goes down again in a circle. The moon does the same, and both are round. Even the seasons form a great circle in their changing, and always come back again to where they are. The life of a man is a circle from childhood to childhood, and so it is everything where power moves.

Havasupai Falls, Arizona.
Spider Rock, Arizona, home to the Navajo's Spider Grandmother.
Shiprock, New Mexico—*Tse' Bit'ai* to the Navajo.
Mount Umunhum in Northern California—resting place of hummingbird by the Ohlone.
Nepal's Machapuchare—holy place for god Shiva.
Japan's Mount Omine—which, until recently, had a ban for women to climb.
Mount Banahaw in the Philippines.
Mountains can be geologic treasures, cosmological repositories to store cultural memory and orientation, not simply fast-twitch attempts to win a summit or plant a flag. Kailash is where Shiva rests. Tamalpais, the home of Coyote. Uluru, Blue Tongue Lizard. As I learn more about this kind of circuitous movement, what's revealed is a shared consensus of care, of restraint, of the Earth not as something to be

owned or claimed. The art of circumambulation attends to something from a distance, a practice accessible to all, one that courts high points without requiring access to their highest reaches. Encircling offers an opportunity to bear witness to a place, a person, or a Self from every vantage point, an honorable surveillance to be with and to fully attend, to accompany every exposure and perspective and behavior of another, analogous to spending time with a close friend or lover and offering presence to all their idiosyncrasies.

The delight when scaling a peak is not necessarily problematic, that euphoric perspective gained when traveling into the vertical realms and working toward a singular goal to achieve it. Summiting mountains is not categorically driven by imperialist motivation, and traveling to high points doesn't have to always entail domination. In fact, some of the most knowledgeable land stewards I know are alpinists who spend much of their lives immersed in challenging landscapes, studying routes and weather, constantly humbled by inaccessibility. But it's also true that I've spent much of my life chasing summits and not knowing why. It was Kailash, and now Tamalpais, that have begun to help me identify the extent to which I had internalized a larger cultural fixation for results, starving a slower and more reverential approach to time and place. Encircling moves in slower motion, and seems to better match foot and breath and intention. Mountains might be lesser served when atomized as single-serving objectives, for to perceive summits or planets or people as useful only when tackled and controlled is to lose sight of a far larger opportunity to belong in an ecology of uncertainty. There is merit in leaving things alone. There is merit in surrender. There is merit in mystery.

STATION SIX | *Serpentine Power Point*

GRAY SKIES LIFT WITH WARMING TEMPERATURES TO reveal the Farallon Islands thirty miles offshore. Islands of the Dead, another settler misnomer. *Ahqa Pilili Walli,* or "the place of churning water," to the Kashia band of the Pomo. Four hundred shipwrecks have met their fate on this archipelago, which is home to the largest white sharks on record, some more than twenty feet long. Wafts of crisping sage drift along the Old Mine Trail as I imagine millions-year-old predators finning through imperial wreckage. Glancing back, I see Laura in sweep and wait for others to pass before violating the silence.

"You're moving strong," I whisper.

"Feeling pretty weak," she says. "Yesterday I felt like dog shit, but I woke up this morning doing a little better." Laura thinks the heat will determine whether she completes this ninetieth lap. She adjusts her rock cairn necklace and keeps walking.

Serpentine Power Point marks halfway, named after a Hopi elder who found this spot to be the mountain's energetic fulcrum, rather than its summit at East Peak. The Hopi honor the sanctity of high country like the San Francisco mountains near Flagstaff, Arizona. Hopi ancestral spirits, kachinas, live on the *Nuvatukaovi,* or "the place of snow on the very top," whose summits are also considered to be the region's water providers. The kachinas must be respected and given proper ceremony in order for them to offer rain for crops, so the Hopi will often make pilgrimages to these mountains for plant gathering and paying reverence. The Navajo have numerous sacred sites around the San Francisco Peaks, too, and both tribes are currently in a legal dispute with a ski resort that makes artificial snow with treated sewage—literally spraying their most sacred mountains with shit.

The name "Serpentine Power Point" derives from a mottled green-blue mineral that's softer than granite but harder than marble. The spine of speckled scales bedazzles the hills, and, as I set my pack down for a sip of mint tea, a four-foot garter snake coils up near my ankle. Here, the route turns inland from the Pacific to wrap around the north side before ascending to the peak. Single-track turns into forest road as we enter Potrero Meadows, where a family of four picnics in the sun. The youngest daughter practices a ballerina spin in the dying grasses, like the Whirling Dervishes, mystic dancing Sufi nomads whose embodied circular meditations came after the poet Rumi visited a marketplace one day in the thirteenth century and became entranced by the hammering of a metalworker, dhikr, a spiritual absorption through repeated patterns. Moved by the sounds of clanking metal, Rumi held out his arms and began to turn on an axis of pure ecstasy, murmuring: "Allah, Allah, Allah." This would later be called *sema*, or divine listening. "Sema," wrote Rumi, "is to struggle with the notion of one's self, like a dying, bloodstained bird, fluttering in the dust."

During these traditional *samazan* ceremonies, the dervish wears a hat resembling a tombstone, *sikka*—death to the ego—and a long-flowing gown to offer a widening shape to the circling. The dancer sheds their jacket and begins to turn clockwise until fully entranced—there are accounts of dervishes lasting more than four hours nonstop. As the dancer spins, the edges of the skirt pull at four times Earth's gravity, their left arm facing down (Earth) and the right arm facing up (God). For Sufis, such whirling is in servitude, to blur lines between Earth and God, an induction of identity abandonment, as one's constricted sense of Self shucks off and the divine rears its crown.

I cross into Potrero Meadows, which Jack Kerouac featured in his 1958 novel, *The Dharma Bums*, where the narrator, Ray, spends extensive time here with Japhy Ryder, a fictional Gary Snyder and real-life friend of Kerouac's. Japhy plans to conduct a walk around the mountain behind his home: "I'm goin to Marin County in a few weeks," says Japhy, "go walk a hunnerd times around Tamalpais and help purify the atmosphere and accustom the local spirits to the sound of sutra." After a three-day bender, the two wander into Tamalpais to sleep in Potrero Meadows. I can almost smell their cigarettes across the meadow as I pass in silence, the glowing ends suspended like fireflies around a smoldering pit. My phantom grizzly returns, too, loping through the fields known every spring to offer wild bouquets of iris.

Kerouac and Snyder were well-established in California's literary pantheon by 1955, following Allen Ginsberg's Six Gallery reading of "Howl," and Snyder's "A Berry Feast." Philip Whalen, Ann Charters, Jack Kerouac, and Kenneth Rexroth were all present, walking in the footsteps of earlier literary legacies like Ina Coolbrith, California's first poet laureate, Mark Twain, Bret Harte, and others. Avant-garde aesthetics, literary experimentalism, civil rights, and sexual liberation all collided along this continental edge. The 1960s saw an era of student protests that began in San Francisco with the real

Black Friday: After a congressional hearing, union-busters broke up students by attacking them with water hoses, hit "like trees in a hurricane" by four hundred policemen. This was the era of Ken Kesey and the Merry Pranksters, the famous acid tests, and the 1966 Trips Festival at San Francisco's Longshoremen's Hall, which summoned tens of thousands of anxious youth. The Grateful Dead played their first choreographed light show to several thousand people, many of them tripping on LSD punch. Later that year, the Black Panther Party organized in Oakland. In January 1967, a Human Be-In held at Golden Gate Park kicked off the "Summer of Love," where thirty thousand people attended, including Snyder and Ginsberg, two of the event's ringleaders, who organized a circumambulation around Golden Gate Park's polo field on the final day. This was the soil in which the Tamalpais walk first sprouted in 1965, in opposition to war and materialism, and toward a different shape of resistance, a counternarrative. A countershape.

Here in the fifth hour, I imagine how different the world must have looked then, how the first Tamalpais walk came into existence during this cultural moment. To conflate political revolution with embodied revolution around mountains might be a stretch, but there's something about the shared language I find revealing. *Revolution* derives from the Latin *re-volvere*, to "revolve back," or "return to" a previous state. The Greek historian Polybius first visualized the shape of change as cyclical: First, you have a tyrannical kingship that spirals into aristocracy, oligarchy, democracy, mob rule, and, eventually, anarchy. Governing bodies, he thought, held their ground but would eventually "return to the point from which they started."

Romans didn't offer much breath to *revolution*, either. Their closest analog was *res novae*: "new things" or "innovations."

Stoic philosopher Marcus Tullius Cicero described political change as an *orbis* (wheel, circle, sphere, cycle), or *convertere*, a "turning on an axis or of rotating." The word *revolution* didn't emerge until the 1500s, mainly among astronomers. Orbiting planets and stars were being vigorously recorded following Nicolas Copernicus's *On the Revolutions of the Celestial Spheres* (1543), his heliocentric model dislodging Earth from center stage. According to astronomists, the earliest revolutionaries didn't wear bandanas or brandish rifles. They were cut from the sky and arcing stars and lobbing moonlight and planetary orbit. *Revolution* imbued a force beyond human will, something driven by Spirit: "Human events and the course of history would follow the same inexorable and fixed schedules as the motions of the stars, suns, moon, planets, alterable by the direct intervention of God," wrote Harvard history professor Bernard Cohen in *Revolution in Science*. "A revolution could arise by man's intervention, transcending or momentarily replacing the inexorable sequence determined by the revolutions of stars."

Hannah Arendt, one of the most erudite political thinkers of the twentieth century, spent substantial time deconstructing the anatomy of revolution as both a political and psychological phenomenon. Arriving to the United States in 1941 after having fled the Nazis, she grew fond of its democratic vision and wrote at length about it in *On Revolution* (1963). Arendt suggested that the primary aim of all revolution is freedom, yet she placed caution on the manufacture of "beginnings" as a significant element of a nation's origin myths, implying an inevitably linear direction of all that follows in the wake of a revolution. Beginnings are something the dominant culture fashions and can be used as acts of violence and erasure. "No beginning could be made without using violence, without violation," writes Arendt. The science fiction novelist Ursula K. Le Guin connects this power with a sort of collective amnesia: "One of our finest methods of organized forgetting is called *discovery*."

Arendt addresses the appropriation of revolution's fixed origins, that we once lived and died as "the stars follow their preordained paths in the skies... that it was only during the course of the eighteenth-century revolutions when men began to be aware that new beginnings could be a political phenomenon, that it could be the result of what men had done and what they could consciously set out to do." She continues:

> As long as men took their cue from the natural sciences and thought of this process as a primarily cyclical, rotating, ever-recurring movement... it was unavoidable that necessity should be inherent in historical as it is in astronomical motion. Every cyclical movement is a necessary movement by definition. The role of revolution was no longer to liberate men from the oppression of their fellow men... but to liberate the life process of society from the fetters of scarcity so that it could swell into a stream of abundance. Not freedom but abundance became now the aim of revolution.

She tacks toward this assertion of abundance, that "to partake in the body politic of the nation, each national must rise and remain in constant rebellion against himself" to become better, echoing the Trappist mystic Thomas Merton when he said, "Life itself is revolutionary, because it constantly strives to surpass itself." Here, compassion becomes the guiding principle.

Arendt's philosophy of revolution met me as I was first becoming obsessed with performing revolutions afoot, routes that invited me into a centrifugal process held together by an unshakable gravity while also being pushed outward, into expanding circles of belonging and stewardship. "Any worldview that makes sense, I think now," writes Paul Kingsnorth, "must orbit around compassion." Ecology whirls everywhere as revolutionary.

And yet, as I continue following Tamalpais around, it still hasn't felt very *revolutionary* in any political sense. But maybe that's the point, for any impulse to overintellectualize pilgrimage, to lose direct witness through such abstraction pulls me away from participating directly in the present moment, an ever-unfolding process void of manufactured beginnings or endings, right underfoot. To practice this style of movement within landscape means dethroning the Self and embracing its connectedness with the rest of life. If Arendt is right—and I hope she is—if compassion is the primary fuel propelling this carousel of political and personal transformation, then simmering at the core of Arendt's mountain is freedom, best when shared, forever in motion, and never won through conquest.

STATION SEVEN | *Serpentine Cairn*

AT 1:30 P.M. THE GROUP BREAKS SILENCE FOR LUNCH AT Rifle Camp. It's taken six hours to feel as if this route has finally begun to wrap its arms around something. While Kailash tethered me to *kora*'s cultural headwaters, Tamalpais swiveled me closer to home, less a tourist seeking something forever outward and now closer to home, and to the Self. Exploring the abandoned camp, I find an old cabin in disrepair. Flipping through my copy of *Mountains and Rivers*, I find Snyder noting a simple structure in his poem: "A neat little saddhu hut built of dry natural bits of wood and parts of old crates; roofed with shakes and black plastic. A book called *Harmony* left there." The three poets stopped here at Rifle Camp for a meal of "swiss cheese sandwiches, swede bread with liverwurst, salami, jack cheese, olives, gomoku-no-moto from a can, grapes, panettone with apple-currant jelly and sweet butter, oranges, and soujouki—greek walnut in grape-juice paste."

My jack cheese and avocado sandwich are poor rations compared to their Beat charcuterie. Oren and Laura sit on opposite sides of the camp to create two groups and I toggle between them, snapping off squares of chocolate for willing recipients. "The word *kora*," says Mike Scott, seated next to Laura and Victor, "it's nice and sweet, but my tongue and lips really like *cir-cum-am-bul-a-tion*. It's worth a lot to me sensually." Victor laughs.

"You just like that word because it brings your mustache to life," Laura says. "When you say *kora*, nothing happens to it. But say *cir-cum-am-bul-a-tion* and that little Mark Twain mustache of yours does a dance." Laura wiggles her hips and the three erupt. There's a sweet camaraderie in this group, compassion for one another that's been tended for decades. I think of Ian Baker's assertion a year ago around Kailash that to perform *kora* with others is to share a current of intentionality, overcoming something that's limiting us, something holding us back. After lunch, the group tucks into silence again to stride toward the seventh station— Serpentine Cairn, a three-foot-tall stone pile accumulated over the years. Oren pulls a chant sheet from his JanSport while Laura recites the mantra from memory. Everyone offers a rock, a prayer. I send mine to my mother.

•••

ONE MONTH BEFORE THE WALK, I TRAVELED TO SAN JOSE, California, to take my mother to her first radiation appointment. After several rounds of chemo, I watched as she adjusted her threadbare, sand-blonde wig in the hospital window's reflection. This cancer had already ripped months from her life, decades in that Silicon Valley apartment watching Lifetime Originals and B-list crime shows with her incontinent terrier, Coco. One evening, the night before a scheduled visit to the dermatologist about melanoma on her back, she tripped over Coco and grazed her breast on the kitchen table as she fell. Mom's sunspots from years of tennis turned out benign but, before leaving, she asked the doctor to take a look at the swelling on her breast, and there he found a tumor the size of a tennis ball.

Mom looked at me in the waiting room. We hugged. I kissed her cheek, cold and waxy like parchment paper. "Everything is gonna be fine," I told her. "Nothing to worry about. Just breathe." I hate when people tell me to breathe. "You're a warrior," I said. "You're gonna destroy this cancer. Gonna kill it. Gonna fuck it up. Gonna win this battle." I found myself using language as if her body were a battleground. She smiled back. What I saw was a tired yet resilient woman in the same body who played on the Wimbledon Grandstand, who rubbed shoulders with Billie Jean King, Arthur Ashe, and Pancho Gonzales, the same body to which I owed everything. Pain scribbled all over her face, fault lines more noticeable now than ever, and my heart expanded in attendance to its every aspect.

People took numbers and waited, holding their fork-tongued slips with red numbers as if queued up at the DMV. "Number eighty-eight?" called a voice in the loudspeaker. Number eighty-eight was the Vietnamese lady seated next to us. She stared into space with her jaw clenched, as if holding in a one-minute scream. Eyebrows, gone. Hair, gone. Fingernails, gone. Skin like olive-splotched cellophane, a hide stretched across bone. "Number eighty-nine?" the nurse called into the waiting room. My mother flinched. I squeezed her hand. She rose with a grunt, then shuffled toward the double doors in her black-and-purple Asics, the kind worn not by world-class tennis players but the ones you buy half off at Ross. It was hard to believe this was the same body that fought it out with the finest tennis players in the world. I remember having slowed down, still, and loving her so much in that moment, a new kind of love—raw and unconditional, neither cinematic nor rushed. The love felt urgent. Shared.

"You're a warrior, Mom," I whispered as she disappeared behind double doors.

I swore I heard her whisper back, "Fuck warriors. Fuck summits."

STATION EIGHT | *Colier Spring*

OM OM KRING KRING SVARUPE
OM TARE TU TARE TURE SVAHA TARE TARE

The mantra that once felt out of place now begins to function more like breathwork. We traverse the remote north side of Tamalpais to the eighth station, which rests by a spring gurgling beneath a redwood grove, and I kneel with cupped palms for a taste next to Laura, who flops to her side. A pair of day hikers arrive from a spur trail.

"Do you know where the mountain is?" one asks.

"You're *on* it," Laura snaps back, before leaning over to me and whispering: "Now there's a philosophical question: Where exactly *is* the mountain?"

To find out where exactly Laura's mountain was, two weeks earlier I had hopped on a train to visit her San Francisco Mission District apartment. Laura lived in a well-worn but colorful and tall-ceilinged place with soft light, where elm branches scratched at the second-floor windows. In her bedroom a painting of Tamalpais hung on baby-blue walls above an unmade bed. The kitchen was narrow with dozens of dark orange jars lining countertops filled and labeled with Chinese herbs and tinctures, the ones cough syrup comes in.

We sat at her dining room table and ate frijole burritos ordered from her favorite taqueria, using pages of the *New York Times* as placemats. Three pieces of fruit lounged in a thatched bowl, not rotten but close, while birds and rugged coastline themed the apartment's art: a crane dipping its water-colored neck; ocean waves crashing in pastels. Laura's office felt anarchic—walnut desk worn at the elbows and mounded in papers; opaque jars stuffed with feathers and rocks; unlabeled cardboard. Tamalpais memorabilia covered one wall top to bottom with photos, postcards, and maps, as if I'd stumbled upon a private investigator with obsessive evidence and mugshots pinned to the wall. The only non-Tamalpais image was a framed photo by George Fiske, taken in 1900, of two women dancing atop Overhanging Rock at Glacier Point, Yosemite. The two women were Kitty Tatch and Katherine Hazelston, waitresses at the park's Sentinel Hotel. Three thousand six hundred feet above the valley floor, the women appear well-dressed, their hands clasped, dancing on the brink of disaster.

"That picture has a story," Laura said. A friend had given her the photograph after Laura had come out about her homosexuality and found swing dancing to be an effective way to meet other women. "I was a really strong lead," she said with a smirk. Dancing offered Laura both community and confidence, something her childhood lacked, so this cliff-edge couple represented a courage to endure. Staying power in the face of death. When Laura was two years old, her mother died in a car accident after the convertible Laura's father gifted her flipped and crushed her instantly. Her father was never the same again, nor was Laura. "I was mad at him because he took my mom away. My father was a broken man. He made choices that were enraging if you were his red-headed daughter."

Laura escaped to college in Santa Barbara, then moved to the Bay Area, following work as a nature educator. In 1988, she was twenty-three the day she met Matthew Davis on Tamalpais after a coworker invited her to something called "CircumTam." Laura began showing up for every walk, rain or shine. After dozens of circumambulations, the two became close, father-daughter close. They would send handwritten reports to each other after every round, but it was the 2012 winter round that solidified their bond. Horizontal rain kept everyone but Laura and Matthew from attending that day, with flooding on most of the route, including this north-side trail where we are walking now, where Matthew had slipped and fell, and Laura was the only one to help him to his feet. The accident prompted Matthew to acknowledge his frailty, and he asked Laura if she'd like to lead the ritual walks in the future. Laura was ecstatic; there was nothing she cared for more. If swing dancing taught her anything, it was that she was a good lead.

But this verbal torch-passing disappeared among a cascade of ensuing health problems. Laura's reaction to chemo worsened, and she could no longer make the full loop. Matthew's leukemia and shattered hip forced him to stop leading the walk, leaving his son, Oren, as the de facto leader, though he no longer lived in the area and didn't have the same lifestyle as his father. Oren bounced from city to city, job to job, marriage to marriage.

"Oren is the prodigal son!" Laura said. I think of Kartikeya, brother of Ganesh, the wayfaring one who lost the mango of wisdom because he looked too far afield. "He used to go on the hike as a teenybopper twenty-year-old, showing up hungover, while every year I was going religiously, *going, going, going,* thinking about the leadership very seriously. Then Matthew couldn't do it and Oren slipped in. He's been leading it ever since."

Why does any of this matter? I thought. Who actually gives a shit about some obscure, four-times-a-year walk few people know about, attended mainly by silver-haired retirees with too much time on their hands? Why bother? It became evident that this walk and this mountain were keeping Laura alive, and that's why she bothered. It had everything to do with the dependability of place it afforded her amid such uncertainty and fear, and how she offered that dependability back to Tamalpais as a devotional practice. Each season, this route offered her an opportunity for a full appraisal of the place and of herself, muddying the boundaries of both.

As I was leaving Laura's apartment, two things caught my eye. As I passed a series of photos framed in the hallway, I saw wedged in the corner of one picture a black-and-white image of Matthew, who'd sustained this ritual all these years, together with Laura on one of their many shared rounds. The two looked related. The second thing caught my eye just before leaving, and it confirmed for me where exactly Laura believed her mountain to be. Taped above the doorway and draped in Virgen de Guadalupe beads was a small handwritten reminder, impossible to miss before stepping into the world, urgently scribbled in all caps with a black Sharpie: THIS IS IT.

STATION NINE | *Inspiration Rock*

WITH EAST PEAK IN FULL VIEW, WE FACE ONE LAST PUSH to the summit. Laura announces she will split from the group to take a gentler approach, forgoing the steep section ahead, "Manzanita Mangle." A few join Laura, while Oren stands with others atop Inspiration Rock, a flat perch where Lake Lagunitas and Lake Alpine appear to the north as siblings, just like Kailash's Lake Manasarovar and Rakshas Tal. I pluck a manzanita berry and roll it between thumb and forefinger like a mala bead. When Philip Whalen, the third Beat pilgrim alongside Snyder and Ginsberg, arrived at this station in 1965, he wrote:

> To the Summit: North Side Trail, scramble up vertical North Knee WHERE IS THE MOUNTAIN?

French surrealist writer René Daumal asks the same question in *Mount Analogue: A Novel of Symbolically Authentic Non-Euclidean Adventures in Mountain Climbing*, a book that was published posthumously in 1952, eight years after Daumal's death at the age of thirty-six. The novel ends mid-sentence in the fifth chapter, which haunts me still. Daumal died in Paris of tuberculosis, thought to have been accelerated by his early use of psychoactive drugs like carbon tetrachloride, a grain fumigant. It was as if he died while the ink dried, reaching for the summit of his own summitless allegory. The novel's incompletion is perfectly suitable, though, as it follows a group of twelve seekers embarking on an expedition led by Father Sogol to a mystical Mount Analogue on a yacht called *The Impossible*. The protagonist's project is to understand the way of the world, the Self, the universe. Mount Analogue is far higher than any known peak, which implies that "its base must be very broad," larger in circumference than Australia. "Its solitary summit reaches the sphere of eternity, and its base spreads out in manifold foothills into the world of mortals," writes Daumal. "It is the way by which man can raise himself to the divine and by which the divine reveals itself to man." Approaching Mount Analogue requires one to see with unconventional eyes. No one sleepwalking through life will ever be able to see or access the mountain.

After extensive preparations, the expedition finally arrives to the base of the mountain, only to find villages clustered here. They begin climbing up the slopes, an ascent they realize will take years, lifetimes even. Perhaps no summit exists! So why climb? Daumal suggests that there's an interior mountain we're all trying to climb. It's right in front of our nose, but we can't see it, not with conventional eyes anyway. The mountain at the center of the world can be viewed only through direct experience, by going there with full devotion, no expectation of take, only through stubborn and unending attendance of its slopes. In a way, we must prepare for this climb to be a never-ending courtship of the world, the Self, divinity not as some god in the sky but something more grounded, something more like humus. Something here. He writes that to properly engage with this Mount Analogue requires a negation of the Self, for we and the crag are indivisibly one, the coordinates of which are available only to those who see with new eyes.

Nibbling on a handful of Medjool dates, I look north from Inspiration Rock and try to view this part of the world where I'd grown up with new eyes. There was a real summit to this mountain, and we were close, but what sort of finality awaited my arrival? Circumambulation complicates such linear fixations, a way of movement Snyder told me was "truly one of the great practices," while it might also act as a ritual for processing grief. He noted in *Tamalpais Walking* that encircling burial mounds marked some of our earliest known origins of circumambulation, a nod to the cyclical nature of mortality. "Part of ancient Indo-European lore, Indo-Aryan lore," he said, "probably goes back to central Asia and includes the Celts."

This kind of grief embodiment by circular walking was expressed most strikingly by the author William deBuys. In the 1970s, he began following the same three-mile loop around his northern New Mexico property in the wake of a failed marriage, and would continue this walk regularly for the next three decades. Chronicled in one of the most wonderfully melancholic books ever written on circumambulation, *The Walk*, with every passing round, deBuys maps an interplay between his heart and the temperament of the Sangre de Cristo wilds. "The landscape abounds with flaws, like those who walk it," he writes.

As I'd been learning about Laura and my mother's cancer, healing for deBuys came in two stages. First, attention was paired with repetition, something predictable and ritualized amid uncertainty. And then deBuys's practice was also one of observation over time, slow, not putting one's head down and shuffling forward, but embracing joy and pain while attendant to seasonality—arroyos parched, arroyos flooded; the night that brought the mudslide; the afternoon a cougar pawed across the meadow; the time he was forced to shoot his arthritic horse Geranium in the head with a revolver. Here, deBuys recounts every detail of this last act with great tenderness after placing the body in the forest, where it was taken quickly by wild creatures and imprinted forever onto his walk. Occasionally, deBuys would invite others on his round, but more often he'd go alone. Sometimes clockwise, other times counterclockwise. The direction didn't matter much. What mattered was the matter, crossing boundaries of inner and outer landscapes to blur the two:

> A dispassionate observer, watching from afar, might say that for more than a quarter century I have been going in circles, round and round the same hill ... I am twenty-seven years invested in making this circuit, in mulling and trying to read the story of a single landscape over a long time, in using the same walking meditation to hear, or at times quiet, the voices inside my head ... I walk or ride a horse, thinking I am going along in a straight line, but then a sound, a glint of light, a stray idea—some tug on sense or mind—and I see I am headed somewhere else: to the boneyard where I shot the mare, to check the dam in the arroyo, to a well-known tree or rocky outcrop, or to no certain place at all. I take the walk, and then the walk takes me.

STATION TEN | *East Peak*

A LOOKOUT TOWER BALANCES ATOP EAST PEAK AT 2,572 feet, like an inverted dreidel wrapped in barbed wire and security cameras. To the south, the bay is busy with ports and boats, highways and traffic, rush hour every hour. Skyscrapers poke through the haze like splintered wood. Somewhere behind a rock, a child cries. I pull out Snyder's book.

> All about the bay, such smog and sense of heat.
> May the whole
> planet not get like this.

Chief Marin. The bleeding cross. Coyote. The view is captivating, but it's clear that this peak is no destination. Human exceptionalism isn't someplace we can stay for long. What am I supposed to see here? Triumph? Horror? Possibility? No, what I see is smog. I see checkered patterns and grids and cubicles. I see combustion and hustle. I imagine the hospital where I was born forty miles south, near to where my mother is now, likely sitting in her apartment eating an omelet topped in Safeway cheddar and expired ketchup as radiation cycles through her body.

How do I actually widen my circumference enough to feel these troubled bodies in my own troubled animal heart? This appears to be the task, though its coordinates remain lodged firmly in my head. Pierre surrendered after facing Kailash with offerings of his dead daughter. Laura embraced her recovery through years of holding court for this mountain pilgrimage. I'd traversed from the Eastern origins of this tradition to what feels like some intersection of Western civilization and hubris, and now what? Where am I supposed to go? "Only when you drink from the river of silence shall you indeed sing," wrote the Lebanese American poet Khalil Gibran. "And when you have reached the mountain top, then you shall begin to climb. And when the earth shall claim your limbs, then shall you truly dance."

OM A RA BATSA NA DE DE DE

After several hours of movement, no one in the group is dancing. The vegan raven-squawker looks worn. The flirtatious park ranger I befriended while scouting the route months ago checks her phone for service to call her boyfriend. Gonnerman, the esteemed Snyder scholar, struggles to stand. Veteran pilgrims Mike Scott and Victor Ichioka remain solid but are ready to close the loop. Everyone adjusts their packs for the final descent to Muir Woods. As Oren passes Laura to leave, she extends her hand for help, but Oren moves too quickly to notice. Instead, I help her up and check to see how she is doing. Laura pats the salt from her temples with a handkerchief and whispers, "I got this."

To the west, the horizon blurs sea and sky with an incoming storm. The Farallon Islands and their shipwrecks and sharks disappear into pillows of fog. To the south, weather covers the Santa Cruz Mountains. As a child, I imagined this marine layer as a slow-motion tsunami overtaking the city, crashing into the bay to reset everything.

Passing by the decommissioned lookout tower, I notice a surveillance camera. *Sur-* ("over") *-veiller* ("to watch"), from seventeenth-century Europe during the Terror of France, where committees were set to track movements and patterns of dissidents. State surveillance gestures at an omnipotent, all-seeing god, ruling from above to correct those who stray far out of line. The kind of surveillance I found in Tibet is among the most comprehensive and sophisticated the world has ever seen. The Lhasa prayer wheel camera. Chinese speed governors. Security scarecrows. The Chinese soldier coming out of nowhere during a routine bathroom stop. I've started to imagine these circumambulations as a kind of countersurveillance, for to bear witness to seasonal change and violation within a landscape requires constant attendance to all that's at stake.

STATION ELEVEN | *Mountain Home*

THE ROUTE TUMBLES SOUTH FROM THE SUMMIT, following a punishing series of railroad ties for stairs toward Muir Woods, through Fern Canyon, and down to Mountain Home, a small ridgeline community. Some had planned to only reach the peak and arranged rides home, and the group is now ten, Laura in sweep. I pass a water tower, ferns growing from its lid as a green hummingbird sticks her beak into the overflow. Coast Miwok consider Hummingbird an important messenger, sent to fetch fire from the Sun. The bird risked her life, but returned with a spark held beneath her chin to warm the community.

Gary Snyder once wrote that circumambulation is "a way to see the mountain with gratitude and attention in all seasons; in a steady circuit which is never the same twice... no longer just a playground or getaway, but a temple and a teacher, a helper and a friend." I sit and watch my pollinator friend, an animated expression of the mountain itself, fly and work and continue on. When we reach Mountain Home, the last station before the finish, light fades and Laura is nowhere to be seen. Oren launches into the Four Vows for Spiral Walkers; I can tell he's anxious to finish. By this point, I pronounce each verse loud and full-throated:

Sentient beings are numberless; I vow to save them.
Consuming desires are endless; I vow to end them.
Bio-relations are intricate; I vow to honor them.
Nature's way is beautiful; I vow to become it.

The vow's final line catches me as silence overtakes the ridgeline at dusk. Nature's way surely is beautiful, and I promise myself to seek to embody these patterns I've been following, patterns I'd found repeating over and over in the more-than-human world. Canines, for example, walk in circles before defecating, as they carry a hypersensitivity to magnetic fields, predisposing them to face north or south. They will circle a location before bedding, too, a practice inherited from their wolf progenitors to mat down grasses and chase off dangerous critters. Vikings documented reindeer cyclones, in which hundreds of reindeer form counterclockwise stampedes around threatened or targeted herd members in order to protect them.

Dolphins are known to swim in circles around those in danger too. There's one story of a cyanotic teenage girl found three miles off the Los Angeles shoreline with a plastic bag tied around her neck, including her passport and suicide note. A group of scientists had been studying dolphin behavior nearby when the pod darted toward deeper water. They tracked the dolphins, which led them directly to the girl's body. The dolphins encircled her until the crew raced the girl to shore. She lived. Then there's Adam Walker, a British endurance swimmer who was attempting to cross New Zealand's Cook Strait, one of the most challenging stretches of water in the world, when he spotted a great white shark the size of an SUV hunting him from several feet below the surface. Within minutes, ten dolphins arrived and began encircling him until the shark lost interest and disappeared into the deep blue.

The phenomenon of the ant death spiral has captivated myrmecologists for years, where nearly blind army ants will form an orbital march, sometimes numbering in the tens of thousands. This behavior was first recorded in 1921, when the naturalist William Beebe bore witness to an "ant mill" 1,200 feet in circumference. One lap took more than two hours for an ant to complete. In *On Trails*, Robert Moor writes that ants and caterpillars will sometimes secrete pheromonal trails for others to follow to a reliable food source. In one study, an entomologist watched ants circling for forty-six hours straight as they moved, entranced, thinking a meal was near. Nearly all died. During East Africa's annual wildebeest migration, two million ungulates—wildebeest, zebra, and gazelle—move along the Serengeti in the largest mammalian circumambulation on the planet, a thousand-kilometer gyre of heft and hackle in search of fresh grasses without beginning or end. Each January, half a million wildebeest calves are born, herds swell, and from this begins a circular pursuit of survival, following available forage. The seasonal rains that produce these Serengeti grasses are charged directly by oceans, which churn in similar cyclicity.

Five oceanic gyres—Indian, North Atlantic, North Pacific, South Pacific—are shaped by many factors, including the Coriolis Effect, which is also the primary architect of hurricanes. The Coriolis is essentially an act of deflection—as Earth turns, all rotation is not equal on the surface of a spheric plane: The speed of rotation at our steamy equator whips faster than at the poles. Heat from the tropics lifts and diffuses north and south—thermal redistribution—and when this surface temperature change meets a spinning planet, the combination turns into gyres and weather.

Hydrological cycle. Carbon cycle. Electrons around a nucleus. Coronary circulatory system. Bodies circulate blood, oceans gyre, hurricanes funnel, ants march, and ungulates follow the seasonality of grasses as celestial revolutions churn above it all. At every level, nature's aesthetic motion is one of unending departure and return, dissolution and resurrection. The more I've begun to see these cyclical patterns in the more-than-human world, the more I wonder if it was my mother's favorite story that may have been what started me on this fixation with circular movement.

In 1968, she had traveled to South Africa as one of the most promising American tennis players, an eighteen-year-old tennis professional alongside Kristy Pigeon, another rising star of the sport. They were invited to the Sugar Circuit sponsored by Virginia Slims, a tobacco company that supported female athletes for their sex appeal, targeting young women like my future mother for profit. In my mother's retelling, the two arrived to Kruger National Park during a rainstorm in a borrowed Volkswagen van with one functioning wiper that smeared rust across the windshield. Her whole life she'd daydreamed about untethered landscapes convulsing in wildness: hippopotamuses, cheetahs pawing across the savannah, hyenas cackling. She loved every bit of it, anything to escape her scheduled life at home, one of discipline and expectation. What she craved most was to chain-smoke on trains to who-knows-where with who-knows-whom, to be chased by boys and be taken by something other than tennis, her first love but also the only identity she had ever known. So when sponsors offered an all-inclusive trip to Johannesburg, including a week of safari with her best friend, she agreed.

Butch was their bush guide for the week, a meat-and-potatoes South African with a steel wool mustache and thick thighs. My mother was in love at first sight. One morning the two young women piled into the back of a jeep with Butch and his field assistants. They traveled the park to track lions and gazelles, African buffalo, civets and aardvark, oribi and reedbucks and unknown bird species. They watched as one lioness perched in a tree to prey on a zebra and leapt from her branch to dig her claws into striped flank. After two hours, the jeep pulled off the dirt road and Butch's face coarsened. In the distance, two zebras, a mother and her child, huddled together on alert. The colt buckled at the knees when the jeeps arrived, hiding behind his mother. It takes only fifteen minutes after birth for a foal to stand on their own, mom would say; within an hour they can run. Pure instinct.

"Gotta tranq' the momma," said Butch, twisting the meat of his torso around in the driver's seat. "Need to move her to a new corner of the park where there's more water. Shouldn't take long." South Africa was experiencing severe drought, and Kruger officials were relocating vulnerable wildlife to other regions of the park, an effort known as "Operation Numbi." Another jeep arrived and three others hopped out shouldering semiautomatics. Butch started to load a dart gun as the sun throbbed. Several men fanned out to form a semicircle around the zebra. The adult's head was cocked, muscles primed for escape. Butch raised the gun and shot. *Flump.* In a second, the zebra released a sound of unalloyed terror while her colt flinched. Butch had lodged a dart into the mother's muzzle. The two split in opposite directions, the mother tore away from the jeep and her child. Butch jumped back into the jeep, started the engine, and began to track her down. After twenty minutes they spotted the mother zebra, collapsed in a heap on the ground. The colt was gone.

"Where's her kid?" my mother yelled, scanning the landscape with binoculars. Everything was moving too fast. They approached the mother as her body convulsed and bucked, legs kicking up red earth.

"Afraid I darted her in the wrong place," said Butch. The tranquilizer had lodged too close to the animal's brain, and they were going to have to end her life. Butch loaded his rifle, real bullets this time.

Yip yip yip!

The colt had found them. From a distance, the colt peered toward his mother at the center of the scene. He had just learned to run, but tried making up for it with a shrill bark. Meanwhile, the mother zebra's eyes had grown fat, white parts bulging, her flank contracting and filling like tides inhaling through every fiber of her body. Butch told everyone to back away, aimed his rifle square at the zebra's skull, and fired. Denise cupped her palms over her ears, deafened by the shot, and ran behind the jeep, crouching in tears. She wiped her face with the handkerchief Butch gave her and returned to the zebra—and three machetes. The African field-workers asked to take the meat home to their families and sell the hide at market, and they began promptly to stab into the zebra's stomach, slitting her from anus to throat. Blood rushed forth, pint after steaming pint, velvet overtaking black and white, as resident scavengers wheeled above, congregating as intestines purpled in the sun.

Yip yip yip!

Denise looked up to see that the colt had come closer now. She never forgets to include how the young one circled and wailed around his mother. Endlessly. Round and round the colt ran, stopping to look in toward his mother, a body that offered him life and was now little more than a heap of guts and stripes. The colt circled and barked, afraid to get too close but too scared to venture farther away, for there was nowhere else to go. This was it.

STATION TWELVE | *Redwood Creek*

TEN HOURS IN, THE FINAL MILE DESCENDS THROUGH AN elder grove of coast redwoods. All remaining light retreats through towering conifers, making them appear much bigger as we approach Muir Woods. Oren and I discuss his father's death and legacy, and it's clear that Oren doesn't want to be responsible for leading this tradition into the future. I understand. To dedicate one's life to some inherited ritual walk requires slowing down and staying put. "Perhaps the most radical thing you can do in our time," San Francisco author Rebecca Solnit says, "is to start turning over the soil, loosening it up for the crops to settle in, and then stay home to tend them." This staying power requires a playbook of commitment and humility, something Laura embodies fully, but I worry about her declining health. Who will keep this tradition alive if she can't? Will footsteps be enough to keep this mountain from flying away?

Returning to Redwood Creek, the seven of us circle up as the last scraps of light trickle through alders. Oren leads one final chant, the *Heart Sutra*. Reciting the mantra, exhausted in full-throated surrender, I look around and do not see Laura, the person I wanted so badly to finish her ninetieth revolution. She must have hitched a ride from the summit, chemo finally conquering her mountain. A Tibetan prayer flag framed by Matthew Davis rests next to a hawk feather upon the creek bed, connecting Kailash and Tamalpais in a single shape of kinship.

•••

THE NEXT MORNING, I WAKE UP IN MOUNTAIN VIEW, south of Tamalpais, sore and bleary-eyed. Tamalpais had visited me in my dream: "Finally, I'm the center of attention," it said.

My phone buzzes, and a text message arrives. It's Laura.

"Got to the parking lot at 6:25pm! The others were going slow so I walked them in."

Astonished, I write back.

"Wait, so you finished?"

Long pause.

"I did! Ninety times around."

Pause.

"Sore legs, happy heart."

Pause.

"Matthew would be proud."

Laura hadn't given up. Gonnerman, the Snyder scholar, had struggled on the last descent, so she stuck with him until the end, through the dark. It was Laura's determination and leadership that propelled her around Tamalpais, that and her love for this mountain. As I pause to steep in her little triumph, my phone chimes. It's my mother. She wants to take me to breakfast and give Coco a bath at the pet store.

"Punch card is full.

Free dog wash today.

Love you."

Lying still for a moment, I let this feeling flood in. I'd been circling around Tamalpais and Laura this whole time, and yet that's not the whole story. Maybe we're all revolving around multiple centers of gravity at once in order to survive, in order to keep loving, to keep breathing. I might be my mother's Tamalpais, or perhaps I'd been revolving around her all along, a colt to his mother, as if only through slowing down the spin and being fully present for Laura's recovery was I able to show up for my mother.

"Yes, Momma. See you soon," I text.

Pause.

"I love you. So much."

Long pause.

"Fuck warriors. Fuck summits."

Peering outside, I face north toward the city. Toward Laura, toward Tamalpais, toward this convergence of East and West. Coast Mountain, a modest uplift of rock teetering at the edge of a tectonic fault line. Fog breaches the mountains and floods the bay, and I imagine the great tsunami. The cycles wheel along. The revolutions persist. The bay is full again.

ROUND THREE | *Pit*

The wind blows hard among the pines
Toward the beginning
Of an endless past.
Listen: you've heard everything.

—Shinkichi Takahashi

ONE | *Home*

FIRST YOU TAKE A LEFT ONTO MONTANA STREET, WHERE you'll pass Iron and Aluminum to meet a third left onto Platinum after the Copper City CrossFit, and if you reach Gold you've overshot your turn, which is to say you must aim for the Travona Mine, next to West Elementary, before hooking a final left onto Diamond Street, because here on Diamond, you will arrive to the midcentury bungalow of Joe and Sherry Griffin. This two-bedroom home in Butte, Montana stamps out of an American dream playbook, its cream shingled sides and two brick columns bracing a covered porch. In the summer, Sherry grows lilies along its front, cuts grass every other Friday, and makes sure there are culinary herbs available for her neighbor, Anna, who sometimes sneaks over to steal chocolate mint sprigs for happy hour. Juleps and town gossip. Porch therapy, she calls it.

The air smells clean. Not like it used to.

Inside the home, art hangs in nearly every room of the house, showcasing Butte's main attraction—the Berkeley Pit. The first image of the Pit is in the living room, a panoramic illustration of the abandoned open-pit copper mine, its industrial spiral-cut layering paired next to a Russell Chatham print of cottonwoods in snow. The second image is thumbtacked in the bathroom, a commemorative poster set in pastels from the "Cool Water Hula" that took place in Butte in 2000. On this day, over a hundred people met at the Bell Diamond steel tower headframe, wearing blue sarongs to perform a "healing dance" to the tune of the Sons of Pioneers song, "Cool Water":

> All day I've faced the barren waste
> Without the taste of water, cool water
> Old Dan and I with throats burned dry
> And souls that cry for water, cool, clear water.

Pacific Islanders found the event offensive, ceremonial appropriation set to a colonizer jingle failing to acknowledge its Polynesian origins. The third Pit hangs in Joe and Sherry's guest room, previously their son's. He'd moved the hell away from Butte the day after graduating high school. In this room, model warplanes lean undusted beside photographs of pilots tipping their caps, and shelves are filled with two types of books—Air Force history and hydrogeology science:

> *God Is My Copilot*
> *The Way of a Fighter*
> *The City That Ate Itself*

Next I find an illustrated map of Butte's underground, an economic geology sheet. Alluvium wash from the Pleistocene. Lake beds of sedimentary and igneous layers from the Neocene. Intrusive and extrusive rhyolite. Post-carboniferous quartz porphyry. Aplite. Faults bisect the map with shaft mines pocked across the city and codified in a legend in the bottom-left corner. But perhaps the most revealing image hangs next to it, a black-and-white photo of a ghost, 1913, Meaderville, a Butte neighborhood where many of the city's Italian immigrants once lived. Meaderville, along with five square miles of the city, vanished in the 1960s, consumed by the digging of the Pit along with several other enclaves to become "The Richest Hill on Earth," one hundred–plus mines extracting $48 billion of metals from the Earth, thus crowning it the single richest city in the known world.

That was, of course, until Butte ate itself.

• • •

SID VICIOUS, THE ADOPTED HOUSECAT, IS THE FIRST TO rise on this October morning. He peels along the kitchen table leg before turning to Joe and Sherry's bedroom—no images of the Pit allowed in there. Instead, a Diego Rivera print hangs above the bed, *Flower Vendor (Girl with Lilies)*, a chica carrying a bundle of calla lilies in her arms, a heft of fecundity amid pressures of unavoidable wilt. Sherry awakens to two empty canteens clanking in her husband's backpack as he slings it over his shoulder.

"Hope you find some brain cells out there," she says, pulling the comforter over her head.

"Love you too," Joe says with a grin.

After lathering peanut butter on wheat toast, he feeds the potbelly stove two chunks of lodgepole and steps onto the porch, into a blood-orange sunrise. Joe drives past a semitruck idling under the fluorescent yolk of a Conoco filling station while an artificial hawk sound screeches through loudspeakers, a deterrent for migrating birds, encouraging them to reconsider landing on the surface of the Pit, one of the largest and most toxic surfaces on Earth.

It sometimes works.

He and Sherry moved to Butte in 1990, and remember the exact hawk species chosen by experts to induce maximum hazing effect. (Sharp-shinned.) Joe also remembers the day employees of the Atlantic Richfield Company (ARCO), who owned the mine, cracked hundreds of shotgun rounds into the Pit to scare off migrating snow geese after scraping 342 carcasses from its surface like a routine pool cleaning. The geese had landed on the water and promptly poisoned their organs from the inside out. And Joe doesn't know it yet, but a month from now he will wake to news of a second die-off, this time a thousand-strong skein. Joe understands the data. He understands the danger, having worked here at the largest Superfund site in America for the past two decades. But today, he will walk directly into its shadow.

I met Joe Griffin in 2014, while attending graduate school at the University of Montana. Working for the university each summer, I led groups of international scholars around the state to learn about American land use policy, and one of our stops was the Berkeley Pit. Joe was our designated guide for the day, a respected hydrogeologist and environmental consultant with trusted chops and a bohemian tilt, a man who seemed to balance engineer and artist, lab rat and hippie brat. What I remember most was the way his whole face smiled. Over lunch we shared our affinities for mountains, running, and poetry, and that's when Joe disclosed his top-secret plan, something I couldn't believe when I heard it. I made him repeat it twice.

He wished to walk the entire twenty-mile circumference of the entire Berkeley Pit complex, including its vast tailing ponds to the north. After tending to this place most of his professional life, the idea nagged at him like gravity, despite two reservations: First, all his colleagues thought he was nuts. No one had ever done it, and no one cared to complete the walk with him, a consequence hitched to the second reservation: Joe was sixty-five years old and time wasn't slowing down, but his body was. It was now or never.

Joe shared his idea and asked if I cared to join. I wondered if this was what I'd actually been preparing for all these years, as if the past decade of circuitous journeys—around the world, Mount Saint Helens, Mount Kailash, Mount Tamalpais—had been setting me up for this final test: co-creating my own pilgrimage around the lip of an inverted mountain, inhabited not with venerable gods but filled with fifty billion gallons of toxic water.

The idea seemed crazy at first. Three years ago, I'd arrived to the base of Kailash, curious about how *kora* might help to inform some cultural countershape, but I found no clear answers, only questions. I also began to see much of the world differently, slower and with more radial attention to whatever the path revealed. Over the subsequent years, I traveled obsessively to track this emergent shape, including a four-day, eighty-six-mile circumnavigation of Peru's Cordillera Huayhuash, a walk around the caldera rim of Tanzania's most active volcano, Ol Doinyo Lengai, or "Mountain of God," the thirty-two-mile Pemigewasset Loop in New Hampshire's White Mountains. I guided trips around the ninety-three-mile Wonderland Trail of Washington state's Mount Rainier. During the opening day of the COP21 Paris Climate Accords, a friend and I conducted a ten-hour silent demonstration from sunup to sundown, in the middle of the university in subzero temperatures, while performing six *kora* rounds every hour to represent the six mass extinctions, the current one being triggered by humans. We went nearly hypothermic.

I felt as if I was starting to go mad. That's when I returned to Northern California and found Tamalpais, Coast Mountain, its circuit that went *in* just as it went *up*, in order to look down and out over a bustling, overcrowded San Francisco Bay Area. I determined that this particular route must include the peak so that we might be able to look out onto the beautiful yet troubled landscape, busying ourselves into obliteration with such speed. This was a central theme I'd come to learn through circumambulation: By staying in an unsustainable, near-constant, hyperspeed motion of productivity, by staying in a forward lean that strives always for more—a destination always set outside of me—my capacity to attend fully, to grieve fully and find compassion for what is right in front of me would remain unmet. And yet I still wonder, was this circular motion actually doing anything to further dislodge the Self from center stage, to widen my circles of belonging? Or was this all self-centered eco-poetics and blathering abstraction? Could this practice continue to help me understand in my animal body the unraveling world and the linearity of human exceptionalism? What, or who, lived at the center of this centrifugal narrative, anyway? Was this, asks Indigenous scholar Tyson Yunkaporta, a reckoning or a beckoning?

As Kailash connected me with *kora* and its cultural taproot, Tamalpais brought it home to the West, some fault line that proved far more personal and political. But neither cast its gaze directly into the unsettling future. Here in Butte, I was beckoned by this toxic pit, as if the very Earth underfoot was inviting me to, as Donna Haraway writes, "stay with the trouble," a self-designed pilgrimage for the Anthropocene. The problem was, I hadn't yet accepted Joe's invitation and already I hated this place. It felt like one of the ugliest places on Earth. Kailash was easy romance, a high elevation Himalayan darling enveloped in otherworldliness, while Tamalpais wrapped itself in Beat poetics and deep ecology verse, headlands watched over by thousand-year-old conifers. But here at the edge of this inky hole, there was little to fall in love with, no decipherable song, and yet somehow, I knew in my body that everything had led me to this moment, to Joe, to the lip of irreversible contamination, and to an inescapable legacy of a toxic cavity burrowed into a troubled planet we both called home.

As he awaited my answer, Pierre's purple Play-Doh suddenly flashed into memory. Laura's Tamalpais mantra, THIS IS IT, blinked in fluorescent pink letters three inches above Joe's forehead. Was I ready for this? Was I ready to stay with this kind of trouble, to arrive to a mountain skinned and filleted in broad daylight, flooded into brackish mirrors of our own reckoning? It had been here all along, beating its drum, awaiting my arrival. The poet Antonio Machado writes:

> When the goldfinch cannot sing
> When the poet is a pilgrim
> When prayer will do us no good.
> Traveler, there is no path.
> The path is made by walking.

TWO | *The Underground*

A GREAT BLUE HERON SPEARS FOR MINNOWS AT THE CONfluence of upper Silver Bow and Blacktail Creeks, and Joe stands in the parking lot next to his pickup wearing a faded yellow ball cap, blue jeans, and a jean shirt. He pinches and pulls an iPad to review our route, which starts and ends here at the south end of the pit, a gash so big satellites can see it from two hundred miles above.

"This route is tricky as hell," he says. "Tricky because there isn't one."

We had originally planned to make it a two-day linkup, bivying a night on the north end, but one week before, Joe changed his mind: "We can do this in a day," he emailed. "I'll feel like hell the next morning but it'll be worth it." In either case, to walk around America's largest Superfund site presents three major risks. First, no one had ever attempted the route, twenty miles around and entirely unmarked. Second, the route requires trespassing, with heavy fines for violators. British Petroleum (BP), parent company to the ARCO, now owns the property, and its grounds are highly patrolled. Third, the route includes several miles of bushwhacking, high-security fences, a crossing of the Continental Divide, and six miles of freeway walking. The attempt felt subversive in a way the others didn't.

"You pack an empty bottle?" Joe asks me.

"Packed two," I say.

Joe, I learned, had a more personal reason to attempt this circuit. Before Butte's mining boom started in the mid-1800s, creeks tumbled freely off the Continental Divide to drain into the Clark Fork River, the Columbia, and, eventually, the Pacific Ocean. Upper Silver Bow Creek is the headwaters, our start and finish point, previously unadulterated until mining operations severed its flow. Today, Joe wishes to circumvent this industrial tourniquet. He plans to walk to the north end, fill a bottle with clean water north of the Superfund, and carry it the remaining ten miles to return it here, thus patching together a hydrological cycle that once flowed wild. Joe wishes to reconnect this broken circuit, if only for one reconciliatory moment. It means everything to him and nothing to anyone else. Except me.

It's 7:28 a.m. when we begin walking clockwise.

•••

"WHAT THE HELL IS THAT?" I ASK, AS WE WALK PAST A twenty-foot wall of black tar the length of a football field.

"Slag," Joe says. "Byproducts after metals were removed during mining and smelted from ore. Metal and silicon oxides, mainly. You'll see this shit heaped all across town."

We cut through downtown as frost clings to eaves and lawns. A pink tricycle with white streamers leans on its side in the yard of a double-wide trailer, left out overnight next to a stack of hula-hoops. Chinatown. We pass the historic M&M bar, where Jack Kerouac had once stopped, later claiming that it was his favorite. It's hard to imagine this city bustling with more than one hundred thousand residents a century ago, a swollen immigrant workforce filling its union halls, newspaper boys lugging headlines of world wars in the crooks of their arms. Only thirty-five thousand people live here today, and the downtown sustains a whisper of convalescence from its muscular, industrial past.

Aluminum Street.
Gold Street.
Porphyry Street.
Mercury Street.
Clear Grit Street.

Storefronts are pulseless as we pass a corner market recast as a liquor shop. I imagine prostitutes puffing hash from its second-floor balcony and peering down on future clientele. Butte's red-light district was known for employing more than a thousand unionized sex workers as Irish, Italian, Chinese, Finnish, German, and other immigrants flooded in with sights set on future prosperity, as if the underground flitted in something sacrosanct. This place promised a bountiful life, a bestselling action novel fast paced and plotted in vice, a Rocky Mountain casino met with a patriotic call to arm the war machine, to *electrify freedom!* with its endless metals, mainly copper.

Long before Europeans arrived here, the *Snt'apqey*, or Silver Bow Creek, offered abundance to the Indigenous Salish, Shoshone-Bannock, Pend d'Oreille, and Blackfoot for hunting and fishing. Butte's settler history starts around the time of California's Gold Rush. As Europeans pushed west in the 1840s, many never reached California, and those who did would find an oversaturation of mining claims and seek their fortunes elsewhere. Butte was a boomtown run by two copper kings—William Clark and Marcus Daly. After early prospectors discovered gold along this creek in 1864, merchant-banker Clark began to invest in regional claims.

Irish-born Marcus Daly arrived shortly after from Nevada's Comstock mine to purchase a $30,000 claim, the Anaconda, referencing a *New York Tribune* article by Horace Greeley on the Civil War: "Grant will encircle Lee's forces . . . and crush them like a giant anaconda."

In 1882, Daly discovered a thick vein of copper, and the timing couldn't have been better. The telegraph and incandescent light bulb technology were just being introduced to the market and both demanded miles of copper wiring. So the two copper barons kept digging. And digging. Montana became part of the Union in 1889, and in less than ten years, Daly's operations ran the state, amassing a tremendous infantry of workers and paid-off politicians. At one point, three out of every four Montanans worked for the Anaconda Copper Company. But such fortunes weren't enough. Clark sought total conquest and tried to buy his way into political and media dominance during the 1899 election. Daly would sell Anaconda to Standard Oil, which owned most all of America's oil assets. By 1915, half of the US copper supply came from Butte. More than sixteen thousand workers called the city home, and Butte's population ballooned to some ninety thousand people, the largest metropolis between Chicago and San Francisco.

As Joe and I cross town, heading north toward Walkerville, the morning air smells of autumn, of burn piles and composting duff. The pit disappears from view, but the haunt of it lingers with every step. Joe points to a memorial near the northwestern edge of the Pit, where the Granite Mountain and Speculator headframes—large triangular steel pulley structures for hoisting metals from shafts below—once towered above town. Several decades ago, Butte was known as an ugly duckling, what Michael Puńke in *Fire and Brimstone* called a city with an "expectation of imminent abandonment." Arsenic smoke hung in the air like a perpetual fart while underground operations proved fatal, averaging a kill a week.

Such hazards came to international attention with the 1917 Granite Mountain and Speculator Mine disaster, the largest hard rock tragedy in US history. In three days, 163 men died after a fire broke out underground. By that time, ten thousand miles of shafts tunneled beneath the city, some more than three thousand feet deep. As the fire ripped through the tunnels, headframes hauled bodies up from below. Young men were stripped naked, charred and suffocated from the heat. Others were found holding each other, a final embrace before their skin started to fuse together. Dozens perished face down in the mud, their knuckles worn to bone after trying to claw an escape through concrete bulkheads a mile underground. Others were steam-scalded to death as rescuers tossed water from above to extinguish the flames.

"Get the rocks in the box. / Get the water right down to your socks. / This bulkhead's built of fallen brethren bones," writes Colin Meloy of the Decemberists, who grew up in Helena, Montana, in the song "Rox in the Box."

The North Butte Fire was an industrial tragedy at unprecedented scale, triggering advances in workers' rights movements. Butte became "The Gibraltar of Unionism," with thirty-eight nationalities represented and a miner's union. The International Workers of the World (IWW) showed up, led by Frank Little, a blue-collar "hobo agitator" and Chicago-based heavyweight, which made Standard Oil nervous. In 1914, The company hired thugs to dismantle workers' demonstrations. One night they broke into a mining shaft, stole boxes of dynamite, and blew up Union Hall. Frank Little would later be found bludgeoned to death and hung from a railroad trestle on the Milwaukee Bridge. By Christmas 1914, Butte's labor organizing was a heap of ash.

Everything changed following World War II, when advancements in open-pit mining technology developed elsewhere and Butte couldn't compete, as the city literally sat atop its wealth. To dig a pit meant to relocate entire neighborhoods, something that didn't stop the Anaconda Copper Company and their hunger for dominance. Six thousand family homes were promptly torn down, entire enclaves removed—Meaderville, McQueen, Dublin Gulch—and Butte's open-pit chapter commenced, breaking ground with the Berkeley Pit in 1955. Over the next two decades, the Pit produced 320 million tons of ore, 700 million tons of waste rock, and enough pure copper to pave a four-lane freeway from Butte to Salt Lake City. The Anaconda Copper Company would eventually fold after Chile nationalized their mining operations in 1971. ARCO acquired Butte's operations to profit-scrap for another decade, before shutting down the nearby smelter in 1980 and, finally, the Pit in 1982. On Earth Day.

The shuttering put an end to the constant pumping of toxic waters. The Kelley Mine pump station came to a halt. It had previously been removing several million gallons daily from underground shafts, and now the mines filled with contaminated water, which also filled the Pit. Seasonal flooding continued to leach heavy doses of toxic metals from the Pit into the Clark Fork River, poisoning aquatic life with a heavy burden of cadmium, arsenic, and mercury. With fish kills and widespread health concerns over a hundred miles downstream, in 1987, the Environmental Protection Agency

(EPA) designated Butte/Silver Bow Creek a Superfund site, the single largest environmental cleanup designation in US history. This toxic hole is 7,000 feet long, 5,600 feet wide, and 1,600 feet deep, and it will be with us now for the next 10,000 years, at least.

As a child, I was obsessed with the underground. Jules Verne's *Journey to the Center of the Earth* sat on my shelf, pages worn from repeat reads. Portraits of him all look the same: wispy white hair, shapely beard, triumphant and imperialist, like someone who only made important decisions and left menial tasks to others. Verne appeared stately but frayed around the edges—picture Sigmund Freud in a bar fight. His name evoked salt spray and octopus tentacles, adventuring through dark seas and deep tunnels, oversized journeys and undersized crews, all pushing forward into the depths of an unknown frontier.

His literary success peaked by 1870—just as Butte began to establish itself—after publishing his best-known novels: *Journey to the Center of the Earth*, *From the Earth to the Moon*, *Twenty Thousand Leagues Under the Sea*. The notoriety crowned him the "Father of Science Fiction," and then, in *Around the World in Eighty Days*, Verne wrote the most well-known tale ever published about circumnavigation, a book that itself traveled around the world in more than eighty languages, making him the second-most translated author after Agatha Christie. It's a story about one aristocrat's bet to circle the planet in eighty days or fewer. US railroad magnate George Francis Train inspired the novel, a real-life hypercapitalist who twice attempted a similar trip around the planet. The novel was an imaginary imprint of the times, global circumnavigation the shape of an expansionist frontier narrative, conquest in an increasingly interconnected world.

During the tedium of my parents' dinner parties, I'd often convert our home's bathroom into an imaginary mining shaft and offer rides. Destination? The center of the Earth. After recruiting several adults, I'd stand by the bathroom's light switch and usher each in with a pair of tighty-whities fastened to my head and a Superman cape Velcroed to my shoulders, holding my mother's tennis racket to swat each butt as they entered.

"Last call!" I'd announce, as if I were a train conductor, my seven-year-old voice cracking with each syllable. "Leaving in one minute. *One* minute! Kiss your loved ones goodbye, because you never know what you might find down there." Once everyone was ready, I'd lock the door and turn off the lights. Smells of Budweiser and Camel Lights filled the pitch-black chamber as the descent began. "Past the crust now, onto the mantle, and soon, the *core*." Narrating each geologic layer as if peeling back an onion, I'd switch the bathroom heater on high, signaled by a red dome light. "Starts to heat up as we get closer to the center." Clinking glasses. Creeping claustrophobia. With a flicker of the lights, we'd reach the end of the line—four thousand miles deep—and it was here, at the core, where my elevator would grow piping hot, adults crammed into a bathroom with the heater on full blast.

"Welcome to the center of the Earth!"

I'd encourage them to look around for a few minutes, to take photos of the planet's imaginary core, before ratcheting a lever and returning to the surface. I'd fade out the heater, its red light puttering to black, and arrive home to Menlo Park, California. By then, the bathroom would reek of armpits and Simple Green, and I'd end each tour with the same line: "Thank you for coming with me to the center of the Earth, face-to-face with a gravity that keeps us all from drifting away." And with the swipe of my cape, I'd turn on the lights, open the hatch, and release my hostages. Oxygen would flood in, and everyone would clap and pile out toward more booze. I'd swat everyone's ass as they exited, using Mom's racket. My wand, her sword.

Thirty years later, it was this childhood wonder that attracted me to Butte's subterranean world a month before the walk, to the city's World Museum of Mining, as they led tours underground. Judging by the museum's name, one might expect a global sweep of geologic history, but everything here centered Butte, a city once known as the center of the mining universe. My guide for the day was "Cincinnati Matt," a Montana Tech geology undergrad from Ohio who looked the part: blue jeans, roughed-up hat with tortoiseshell sunglasses rested on its bill. Cincinnati Matt looked more excited about lunch than to talk rocks with our group of six.

"Did you know that, in 1914, nearly 80 percent of the world's copper came from Butte?" he said, kicking dirt and adjusting his cap before droning on about copper's ten-thousand-year history of human use, pendants found in northern Iraq dating back to 8700 BCE. Copper was pliable and plentiful, and for centuries it was traded alongside many other goods in Europe, North Africa, and Central Asia, though other metals were more coveted during this time. It wasn't until the US Treasury began minting copper coins to replace bronze ones that everything changed. Three mothers in the group asked questions about pioneers and engineering and the profiteering annals of extraction. Nothing about displaced Salish. Nothing about the war machine that gave rise to this place. Nothing about Superfund. This is how we look away.

Their children had no interest in this history either, and played tag under an aspen tree as we followed Cincinnati Matt to the underground portal, a corrugated metal tube set diagonally into the hillside and wide enough to swallow a school bus. One mother leaned over to apologize about her kids, but I welcomed their play as it distracted me from this boneyard of rusted nostalgia, backhoes and trolley systems and steel ingenuity, reconstructions of a mining town trying to relive its heyday like some washed up high school linebacker.

After entering the underground, Cincinnati Matt swung the portal shut and locked it. Pitch black, except for headlamps. We would travel just sixty-five feet below the surface today, nothing compared to the ten thousand miles of abandoned tunnels cut below and spread in every direction. I imagined this byzantine network flooded with iron-red water and navigable only by scuba, following an imaginary orb through this netherworld as the entire weight of the city bore down from above.

A miner's ballad tacked to the tunnel wall:

My sweetheart's a mule in the mine
I drive her with only one line
On the dashboard I sit
And tobacco I spit
All over my sweetheart's behind.

The bestial tune held up a middle finger to the Anaconda Copper Company, known to brand their mules in the ass. To spit on their hindquarters was to deface company property. Miners starved these mules, blindfolded and flipped them vertical in cages to be lowered thousands of feet into shafts, where the animals would spend their lives hauling ore through tunnels in the dark. The mules never saw the light of day and most went blind, though some habituated to this back-and-forth extraction and would sit down in protest, unbudging once they had worked their eight-hour shift.

This version of the underworld complicated my childhood love for Jules Verne, for his fictional imagery proved warm and inviting, while this reality felt like a catacomb, like being swallowed by a snake. What had electrified the nation, what offered such light and connectivity, came from this hidden, wretched, dripping dark. The same might be said today, fossil fuels embezzled from these shadowlands and set to whirl aboveground for the express benefit of humans. Though Butte's copper boom is now largely defunct, renewable energy barons are calling upon copper and other precious metals as solar and wind farms require millions of pounds of wiring, generators, cables, and transformers. To connect solar amps to municipal grids requires heavy demands of conduction—a well-designed solar photovoltaic plant, for example, might use nine thousand pounds of copper per megawatt. Copper wiring averages five times more in quantity for renewable systems than traditional energy sources, and most of today's copper is mined in Peru, Mexico, and Indonesia, transported to a global market requiring fossil extraction.

But Cincinnati Matt didn't cover this. Instead, we continued through the tunnel, sharing a scripted history of the many explosives, the evolution of drill bits, spiral cuts. At one intersection, we turned off our headlamps and stood there entombed in a sea of black. I followed the disembodied sounds of children whimpering and mothers apologizing as

I balled my fists in thinking that, as we conquer mountains above, these tunnels invert that dominance, reaching into shadows for the take. Clearly, we are not supposed to stay at the top, or at the bottom, of these tombs for long. These are lonely places, exposed and inhospitable. I stood in the dark as a chill washed over me, offering a whisper of courage to return back to the surface, to oxygen, to living things. We eventually clicked on our headlamps and followed Cincinnati Matt back to the portal to the place above, shimmering with animacy and fire.

THREE | *Trespass*

AFTER THE FIRST HOUR, JOE AND I FOLLOW UNMARKED dirt roads lined in quaking yellow aspens, two miles north of uptown. Smells of a burn pile waft nearby. He stops at a fence stapled with a sign: "No Trespassing, Private Property," below a surveillance camera watching us from a telephone pole. "*Trespassing*," Joe says. "Now that's up for debate." Joe is referring to the false treaties and attempted removal of the Salish, Shoshone-Bannock, and Blackfoot tribes that lived in this region for several thousands of years before European contact. As our boots thud to the other side of the fence, a white truck approaches. "Security guard coming. Hide. *Now*." Joe darts behind a sage thicket and lies on his stomach like it's a military drill. We remain low and out of sight, huddled in the brush as the vehicle passes.

As I bury my face in the dirt, I begin to notice a pattern of surveillance that's followed me along each of these rounds. The Chinese security scarecrows and hidden prayer wheel cameras in Tibet, extensions of the largest surveillance state on Earth. The camera fixed to the top of Tamalpais, watching over the Bay. Every time I'd see a camera, it made me wonder about attention. Moving circuitously had become its own panopticon countersurveillance, something the British writer and "psychogeographer" Iain Sinclair explored in his book, *London Orbital* (2002). Sinclair embarks on a 250-mile walk following London's M25 freeway, one of the world's largest "ring" roads that follows the entire city's circumference. He'd grown concerned about London's socioeconomic disparity and was curious what truths might reveal themselves if one were to walk the lip of a city hollowed out by corporate interest.

Sinclair's observations felt *The Rings of Saturn* Sebaldian, his attunement to the city's surveillance apparatus being the most compelling parts. Whenever Sinclair spots a camera, he imagines it as a head skewered to a stick. He defines an untrusting authority in the middle and the M25 as a "security collar fixed to the neck of a convicted criminal," ground-truthing a city planned on exclusion, its unwanted classes exiled to the edge while the aristocratic elite occupied its core. As Sinclair walks the 250-mile route, he enters a fugue state and his prose swirls in its own quicksand. Buoyed by friends and poets, he passes through cemeteries and churches, into mildewed pubs, and over illegal bridge crossings, charting a path that duels in awe and misanthropy, to compose a pedestrian appraisal of London's soul.

The author finishes *London Orbital* with a realization that maybe he isn't following the M25 freeway at all, his footprints instead performing a kind of death ritual. By engaging with a place's outer edge, the itinerant reveals London's true shape, one designed around fear, to keep the dispossessed far enough away to scrutinize the lordships' kleptocratic core, where elites might forget marginalized communities entranced by the speed of circular five-lane freeways. "The circuits become the treadmills that drive the Blakean geometry of London; spiral vision that finds their deranged resolution in Margaret Thatcher's orbital motorway." Ultimately, *London Orbital* is a call to arms, reminding us that we must remain loyal to the truth, even as those hungriest for power inhabit this mountaintop of loneliness, a toxic solitude.

"As the sun travels around the earth daily in a circle, it impresses on the winds—which contain the breath of God—a similar circular motion, this moving air is breathed into man, reaches the blood, and from the heart the spirit of life is thus carried around the body in an imitation of divine circularity," writes Sinclair. "All walks contradict the lie of the land; they will be circular."

• • •

THREE HOURS INTO THE CIRCUIT AND FULLY TRESPASSING, Joe and I walk in silence—just like the first half of Tamalpais—in order to keep a low profile, contouring the northern arc of the loop and the tailing ponds, where we lose sight of the Pit. There won't be another look at it until the Continental Divide. A beaver dam blocks one drainage, terraced alder-gnaw slowing the water's downstream fate. Through binoculars, I peer south to another dam, this one human-built, a 650-foot terraced berm that separates these tailing ponds from the Pit. The immediate shoreline shifts with life: a flush of whitetail, droppings of elk, tussle of red fox. It feels stubbornly animate despite the violation, despite three rifle shots that crack in the distance, reminding me that it's prime pheasant hunting season. Cloud cover thickens the mood. One section cliffs out, forcing us to heel down to the pond's edge in clear view of authority now, where we tack along a service road next to the tailings. No birds. No whitetail. No fox. Only bouquets of pale mullein and black witch's fungus cluster along the bank, nature doing what it can to sequester life to the surface.

At one turn the road tapers to nothing, eroding into the tailing pond, *The City That Ate Itself*, a landscape of self-harm, an ecological "sacrifice zone," a phrase extended to the human communities here in Butte/Silver Bow County, with one of the country's highest per capita suicide rates, double that of the national average. Though disproportionately male, suicides among women are rising here, too, while Indigenous communities continue to experience the highest per capita rates of self-harm. "It's [enough] to keep our head above water, to keep our kids in clothes and hot lunches," a mother said in an investigation of Butte's suicide epidemic. Chronic pain is a main driver, which can lead to abusing prescription drugs like oxycodone. Eighty-two painkiller prescriptions are written for every hundred Montanans. Chronic pain leads to chronic drug use leads to chronic depression—more than a third of Butte's residents show symptoms of depression—thus completing a vicious cycle that exhumes profit no longer explicitly from the depths of the Earth, but from the underworld shafts of the psyche. The pharmaceutical industry pocketed $1.25 trillion in 2019, profiteering that makes the copper kings look like children in a sandbox fighting over plastic shovels.

Reasons for Butte's runaway rates of self-harm remain opaque, but experts agree that it comes down to sustained socioeconomic hardship, pervasive opioid addiction, geographic isolation, and unmet intergenerational expectations, children not "doing better" than their parents. Here an inherited cultural bootstrap mentality encourages people to privatize anguish, to shove darkness underground where it belongs and get back to work. *Butte Tough. Butte, America*, residue from its mining origins, a fetishizing of the underworld as nothing if not transactional. Now that mining here is nearly nonexistent, avenues for developing a new sense of collective identity are beginning to shift.

"The words I often see when I review suicides," one psychiatrist noted, "is that the person thought they were a burden."

Burden, verb: Old English root. A load which is borne or carried.

Overburden, noun: inert waste or spoils from the soil that lie above a geological feature of commercial significance. Like a copper vein.

Interburden, noun: unprofitable material between two areas of economic interest. No purpose. Expendable. Erase the burden. Hide it away. Dump it into the tailing ponds, out of sight. Value identified and extracted with surgical precision, waste left for others to clean up.

• • •

"This is as good a spot as any," Joe says as we approach the north end of the ponds. Ten miles and halfway around, his limp has downgraded to a hobble. I share the fatigue, but the hardest part remains around the bend. Joe slings off his pack, grabs his canteen, and slides into a willow patch beside the creek, where he dips it into the stream, looks back at me with his water raised high, and turns his whole face into a grin.

Step one: complete.

I follow Joe's lead and draw close to the creek's edge, dipping my bottle into the water and capping it with mumbled prayer.

Endings feed beginnings.

Pierre's pocket of his dead daughter.

Endings feed beginnings.

The tumor fastened to Laura's brain.
Endings feed beginnings.
My mother's breast cancer.
Endings feed beginnings.
Joe's bottle of nontoxic water.
Endings feed beginnings.
Nearby, a pump station clicks on to begin its scheduled treatment.

"You know the process of treating this water will go on into perpetuity." Joe says, the word shrapneled in p's and t's. *Perpetuity*. With constantly rising pit waters and Montana's harsh climate, if rising waters were to carry toxins downstream again, as they did in the 1908 floods, restoration efforts here would be worthless. According to PitWatch, Butte's leading local citizens education group, the "protective level" where pit water must be kept in order for it not to contaminate Butte's groundwater is 5,450 feet. In 1994, the EPA and Montana's Department of Environmental Quality required this line to be held at all times. This included diverting schemes to minimize overflow, as well as constant pumping and treatment protocols. The Berkeley Pit currently holds fifty billion gallons of toxic water in its bowels, water that enters primarily from the bedrock aquifer just below the alluvial groundwater. This system defines the "protective level"—insofar as contamination stays below this threshold, Butte's groundwater remains intact. Even so, all of the city's drinking water comes not from local water sources, but from three outside locations: the Big Hole River and nearby Moulton and Big Creek Reservoirs. The point here is that all water pumping and treatment must continue into perpetuity.

I peer beyond the pump house into the tailing ponds and imagine this hole as if it were an impact crater from the

K-T extinction, sixty-five million years ago. Instead of some fireball angled from above, this particular asteroid emerged from below. Why would a planet burden itself by giving rise to its own annihilation? Why would this planet orchestrate self-harm? It's not until this lap around the Pit that I begin to fully understand this legacy in my body, that a few generations of elite power brokers set into motion an impact we all now inherit and have continued at top speed with extraction and hyperwealth. I am Pit. I am the asteroid. I am the cataclysm burdened from the crucible of Earth's core to bring on the storm. But perhaps I have also been delivered here to bear witness to that storm, to learn through repeated heartbreak and awe that what is good for the land is good for me, and that the inverse is also true. We are the asteroid, forced to bear witness to our own impact crater, tasked now with tending to what dignity remains along this cratered rim.

"Wanna hear something a little woo-woo?" Joe says. "I often imagine this pump station as a postapocalyptic monastery, like after a nuclear event or asteroid strike or a major die-off, where monks will be stationed here to live out their lives in retreat, practicing and tending to this pump for the good of the planet."

I peer back at Joe's postapocalyptic pump house and imagine two saffron-robed stewards pacing out from their station-turned-monastery. The monks appear calm and resigned, each step known, a pace calculated, hands folded behind their lower backs like napkins—one palm wisdom, the other grief—knowing that any previous violations must now be accepted, tended to, and never repeated. One monk bends over, flicks a gauge, and continues on, while the other turns a valve to connect a pipe snaking off to another water treatment center monastery, where more monks congregate, more pray and tend to what remains.

Joe's imaginary pump house doesn't surprise me after getting to know his story. The man was born in Washington, DC, in 1950, an only child whose father was a pilot in the Second World War. The Griffins lived in Virginia for two years before moving north to Cambridge, Massachusetts, after his father was sent to Harvard Business School.

"My dad was a purebred Okie," Joe tells me. His father had grown up in Pauls Valley, Oklahoma, and would take Joe on hunting trips there as a boy. His mother was a city girl born of Bulgarian immigrants. She leveraged an English degree to teach elementary school her entire life, and Joe would inherit a love for poetry from her. By the time Joe turned five, the family relocated to Southern California, zigzagging the Los Angeles basin to accommodate various military assignments. In Redlands, two hours east of Los Angeles, Joe would spend afternoons roaming the fragrant orange groves that checkered the land. Joe was a rebel teen who didn't much enjoy school, so his parents decided to straighten him out at the Sterling School for Boys in Vermont.

"I was too much of a fuck-off."

Joe's saving grace was running and cross-country skiing, which placed him in regular contact with wild space. He recounts afternoons stripping off his school uniform with friends and sprinting bare-assed through the countryside, and his Nordic skiing career coming to an indefinite halt after he showed up to a race tripping hard on acid. "Came on pretty strong near the end," he says with a laugh.

Throughout high school he worked a job building wooden ladders, and his boss would mention how remarkable Montana was. Grizzly bears! Wilderness! And hippies! FM radio had just started taking over the airwaves when Joe tuned in to an advertisement: The Band was headlining a festival in Montana. Joe bought a one-way Greyhound ticket to Missoula and never looked back. When he started at the University of Montana in 1969, the first morning of class he strolled through campus and peered north into miles of wilderness.

"Say, what's past those mountains?" he asked a passing student.

"There ain't shit back there for hundreds of miles," said the student.

This place was unlike anything he'd ever seen in California or New England, wildlands unfurled forever, run by predators and four seasons. Joe bounced between forestry and fine arts, which brought him into contact with three immediate loves: wilderness, geology, and his future wife, Sherry. Sherry Vogel grew up in Bozeman, three hours east of Missoula. A bookworm who majored in forestry, Sherry loved pine trees almost as much as she did poetry, and Joe was smitten from the gun. She graduated and moved to Gainesville, Florida, for work. Joe followed. He found a job there as an environmental consultant for oil drilling and mining sites. Joe was a geology nerd who preferred hands-on work, so consulting paid well and kept him outside, and close to Sherry. After five years, Joe's employer opened an office in Butte, Montana, and his boss urged him to apply. Joe landed a job as well monitor for the Old Works in Anaconda, a now abandoned smelting site that had once serviced Butte in its heyday. Sherry and Joe left Florida in 1990. They would never leave Montana again.

Butte's allure was clear for Joe. The town sat in the crosshairs of geology and public lands, which brought tension to his career, for he had spent most of his life outdoors—hiking, fishing, cross-country skiing on acid—but ARCO was now his employer, one of the single largest polluters on the planet. Joe learned that Butte was a fraught place, the Pit only the visible portion of a complex subsurface tangle of groundwater interactions belowground. For much of his career he apprenticed with leading experts in the area, eventually becoming the lead monitor for the Pit's flood dynamics. It was only through analyzing these large data sets that he really began to notice Earth's patterns, the language, the song.

Joe welcomed Butte as home, but Sherry wasn't so sure at first, for she had grown up in Bozeman and spent her entire childhood snubbing it as a hellhole of fistfights and drunks. It took only a few months before she found her hackles raised whenever people would pin Butte as a cultural backwater. But their investment in this place grew over the years. Sherry would give birth to their son, and Joe toggled between corporate consulting and community water safety initiatives. After twenty-six years, they'd found home in a most unlikely place, someplace full of contradiction, beauty, and desecration, a place they grew to love and steward, despite its challenges.

FOUR | *Madness*

WHAT REMAINS OF THE LOOP IS AN OFF-TRAIL SCRAMBLE over the Continental Divide, followed by a four-mile stretch of freeway that will slingshot us back to town. Though the Pit closed operations in 1982, the nearby Continental Mine remains operational—copper and molybdenum, mainly— but drifting any closer would relocate our walk into the back of a police car. After scrambling up the side of a mountain cleft using saplings and granite nubs for leverage, we tuck behind a rock outcropping for lunch. From here the steep incline tells a deeper story of geologic uplift, sixty-eight million years deep, tectonic plates that shuffled beneath our feet as the great Western Interior Seaway cut the continent in half. This crust drew up toward cool surface temperatures above as it was repelled by heat from the mantle below, a geothermal tug-of-war.

Beneath where we stand, magma continued its heave from below, flows and pilings distributed everywhere, to the point where volcanic material formed a mass extending three miles thick and a hundred miles wide. This magma would firm into place and grow covered in soil, entombed as a subterranean hulk the size of Tennessee—the Boulder Batholith. Today, protrusions of this batholith poke through the surface, while most of it remains underground, settled alongside another mass of cooled magma called the Late

Cretaceous Butte Quartz Monzonite. Large veins of igneous fissures and hydrothermal pressure release valves continued to send heat up from below. Lighter, flimsier minerals like copper and silver accumulated and were trapped in oxidizing ducts, where they nested for millions of years.

Standing on an overlook spooning gobs of leftover tikka masala and jasmine rice from a mason jar, for the first time I can see the full route: Downtown. The Pit. The tailing ponds. The 650-foot dam. Joe's postapocalyptic pump house. The Continental Mine. *There's so much beauty in all this terror,* I think, hating myself for thinking it. The Industrial Sublime. It all feels so wrong and yet so simultaneously harmonic. I imagine this place as one living, breathing cell replete with all third-grade biology class functions: Mitochondrial roads shuttle dump trucks to remove waste; cytoplasm and ribosomes as tailing ponds for storage; warehouses pulverize rock to access their energetic payout, its lysosome; and the nucleus in the middle, the Pit, an eye around which spins a dark seed full of sulfuric acid, deep-frying anything that comes too close. For the first time, by slowing down, I am able to see the true circumference: a mountain turned inside out, quickly conquered and abandoned.

To spit out a seed this big will take time, geologic time, but a pit can be a lot of things. A pit can be a hole, a cavity, a place to hide, a place to die. Old English *pytt*, "water hole"; pit grave, from the Proto-Germanic *putt-*, "a pool." In the 1650s, the word *pit* described evil underworlds meant for exile. As opposed to the upperworld ascension of gods and venerable spirits living atop summits or cloudcaps, evil ones slithered up from nether pits. Pits punch guts. A ring of pit bulls. Industrial Pittsburg. Throw away the pit. Swallow the pit and wild sprouts might grow from your mouth. Pits seethe. Pits smell. Those infernal pits, dank pitted pockets where ticks feed. A pit is a stomach when danger looms nearby. Pits are venues to fight, to mosh, floor-level tickets earmarked for punker serfs. In Greek mythology, Tartarus was the great underworld brokering all of life's torment and suffering, a prison but also a deity. At the depths of Dante's *Inferno*, his inverted circumambulatory descent ends in a portal through the bottom and out the other side. "The Pit and the Pendulum," Edgar Allen Poe's famous 1842 short story, told of a prisoner held during the Spanish Inquisition, strapped down and staring at a lowering blade soon to fillet him. Rats come to his rescue and gnaw the captive free, only for him to be forced toward a seething pit. Pits can be homes to beasts, the million-toothed Sarlacc, jaws held open to the sun in the Great Pit of Carkoon.

But pits also offer kernels of wisdom. A pit can carry a fruit's stone, a life-giving progenitor you tongue in your mouth, too hard to crack. Without a pit the fruit cannot flesh. *Mandorla*, Italian for "almond," the diamond shape formed when two worlds overlap, the marriage of human and divine in its slivered middle, where inner becomes outer, mountain becomes pit, pilgrim becomes path, the surveilled now surveils, and everything points inward and outward into a center that includes everything. "I began to understand that the goal of psychic development is the self," writes Carl Jung in *Memories, Dreams, Reflections*. "There is no linear evolution; there is only a circumambulation of the self. Uniform development exists, at most, at the beginning; later, everything points toward the center."

⋯

"We made it!" Joe says. "The crest of the continent."

After an hour of bushwhacking, we reach the Continental Divide, 7,200 feet, our route's high point. Rain clouds darken and wind vaults thirty miles per hour across the backbone of North America. Within a thumbnail of difference, water drains either west to the Pacific or east to the Gulf of Mexico. We've reached Rampart Mountain, which towers over the entire Superfund complex to surveil a story versed in deep time: the time of erosion; the time to build a planet, a brain, a human heart; the time for mountains and rivers to form; the time for beaver steppes to mound; the time for our curious species to emerge and poke their fingers in soil and find shiny deposits wedged in thermal vents and name it "profit," and, in less than one hundred years, leave a hole that will require constant tending for hundreds of generations.

But maybe even that is inaccurate, for this place won't persist forever. After we are long gone, the Pit will eventually fill and flood and drain and poison everything downstream, until it flows into another restart. I am constantly reminded by these circumambulations that every path is cobbled in bone, perpetual beginnings and endings, and to steward such ecological violation at this hyperobject scale is something we've only recently been able to set into motion—ocean acidification, climate change, nuclear waste storage—all of it offering mirrors to our own hubris. These pits are perhaps necessary to see our shadow selves more clearly. Shadow zoos.

David Abram writes in *The Spell of the Sensuous*: "To Indigenous, oral cultures, the ceaseless flux that we call 'time' is overwhelmingly cyclical in character . . . Time, in such a world, is not separable from the circular life of the sun and the moon, from the cycling of the seasons, the death and rebirth of the animals—from the eternal return of the greening earth." Here, Abram suggests that to think ecologically is to "find oneself in a world of cycles within cycles within cycles," which, I realize now, is what's at the core of this two-decade obsession with walking in circles. It has taken me this long to begin locating myself nested within these cycles, a seasonality subversive in its contention with the linear-dominant narrative demanded by modern life and mirrored back here, along the Berkeley Pit's rim. I've only begun to hear this old geologic song. I've only begun to dance.

We descend from the high point following transmission lines that guide us thousands of vertical feet to the valley floor, opposite the Pit, where a headwind bellows in our merging afoot onto the I-15 freeway, the most dangerous stretch of the route. This is the safest way to link back to town without staying on the ridge, which would draw us too close to the Continental Mine and likely put us in jail. Found objects along the freeway:

> one shit-encrusted diaper
> seven plastic Fireball whiskey bottles
> thirteen Keystone Light beer cans
> six Monster Energy drink tallboys

Uppers and downers. How we love expediency. How we love getting off by getting going. This pace feels mad, even though walking in circles has also been historically attributed with going crazy. In Vincent Van Gogh's painting, *Prisoners Exercising*, the Dutch painter created what would be some of his final works, full of dread and psychosis after a May 1889 admission to the Saint-Paul Asylum in

Saint-Rémy-de-Provence, France. In these paintings, prisoners walk clockwise in a courtyard of brick walls that extend up and off the canvas. Three windows appear out of arm's reach above three guards that preside over the swirl. The windows tease a certain liberty, unreachable escape from a hamster wheel of captivity. But then there is a fourth window. This portal floats on its own above the painting's central character, the one who looks directly at the viewer—a ginger-haired man sagging in jaundice, remnants of Van Gogh himself. The painter was severely depressed at the time; records show that it was unsafe to leave him on his own. Van Gogh completed this *Prisoners' Round* after viewing Gustave Doré's drawing *Newgate Prison Exercise Yard*. Whereas Doré's work was black and white, Van Gogh splashed color on these walls, radiating a sense of freedom.

Today, circuitous foot travel in prisons is common practice. Inmates will "spin the yard" for exercise, release, to socialize, or to follow a bad visit from family and think it away. This semiotic walking fills the inmate with a feeling of moving forward, of progress, of going somewhere, even while accepting it as mere illusion, for there is nowhere else to go. One prisoner for the Marshall Project, a nonprofit that publishes stories from within the US criminal justice system, wrote about the practice:

> I followed the line to go outside to the yard, a few bare acres consisting of a dirt track surrounding an inner oval of sparse brown grass. The track was rutted by men walking in circles for days and months on end; the ruts, trudged by innumerable feet, were full of water from the morning rains . . . Once outside, I had to stay there for the duration of the hour and a

half allotted for recreation. So I joined the walkers ... Walking around in circles is what you make of it. It can be listless and tedious, purposeful and focused, or meditative. I have, as have all prisoners, become expert in walking circles. I first began training to walk circles when I was in a mental-health facility after threatening suicide. I wandered around, in circles and circles, quoting all the poetry I could remember, trying to find the mind and self I seemed to have misplaced.

When living in Portland, Oregon, I sublet a beige studio apartment near the edge of Portland, Oregon's five-thousand-acre Forest Park. Each morning, I'd commute to work and pass Ross, who walked in a circle around a small patch of sidewalk outside the entrance. Ross's revolutions were eight feet in diameter and his pace was always ferocious. With a peripheral gaze through crooked wire glasses, he high-stepped as if treading through tall grass. He always wore the same white tennis shoes, ripped t-shirt, tube socks, and pleated shorts, the same disheveled look as he went on living in a never-ending eddy. Either Ross had already gone mad, or this walking kept him away from the cliff edge of psychosis.

For months, I would leave and return to work, and he would be there circling. I began to say hello. Ross would reply in kind. Though he rarely looked up from his trance, the man knew exactly who was leaving and who was coming, who was heading to work and whose car lock beeped. Ross knew everything, a pilgrim going nowhere and a consort to all, human surveillance spun to the fulcrum of his own psychic instability. He told me several months after I moved in that he'd suffered a mild brain trauma and was placed in our apartment building by his family.

Some days I'd come home with my girlfriend from dinner or weekend adventures and Ross would be there walking, filing every bit of information along with the dozens of other tenants. I'd find myself watching transfixed from my window at night as he spun, where he'd occasionally stop his rounds to stare into the void, the whole world seeming to hold its breath. Then he'd start up again. I finally mustered up the courage to ask him why he walked in circles, why he wouldn't just take his steps a few hundred more yards to the forested trails next to our apartment.

"Everything I need is right here," he told me. Ross figured out something I wasn't able to see, that the world's precious diamonds could exist here in present tense. It was also true that Ross carried a mandate from his psychiatrist not to drift farther than two hundred yards from the property for fear of hurting himself or others. But I never thought Ross to be dangerous. The man never once smelled of booze, but he reeked of body odor, concealed by a threadbare white shirt two sizes too big.

One autumn day, everything changed. I had returned from work and Ross was there to greet my arrival, creating an oval on a sidewalk otherwise covered in yellowing gingko leaves. But something was off. His orbit appeared slower. His half grin was absent. His vertebrae grew sharp at the nape. Ross mumbled to himself from chapped lips as he circled, and it wasn't until I got closer that I saw a deep red-white gash on the left side of his forehead. My first thought was that he had fallen, but upon further review, I'd catch Ross scratching it and noticed that his fingernails were full of blood and skin. With every lap, he'd talk to himself around his private pit, a gravity that had kept him alive all these years but that was quickly coming undone.

"You good, Ross?" I said.

"Oh, hello, Nick," Ross responded in monotone. "How was work? You run in the forest today? What's for dinner, black bean quesadillas again?" Something in his voice plucked a minor chord. Schizophrenia or misplaced meds or a night of hard drinking and depression—all of this was possible. I swung wider around Ross's orbit that day and never saw him again. No one knew what happened. Rumors surfaced that he slit his wrists after trying to hurt someone and was taken away to a psych ward, but I never believed that. Of the hundreds of tenants crammed into that building, Ross was the only one who cared to ask my name. But Ross bottled up a private truth until his centrifuge spun him to who knows where, skull throbbing and bloody-nailed. His center could no longer hold.

FIVE | *The Return*

AFTER AN HOUR OF WALKING ON THE FREEWAY, BUTTE comes back into view as the round enters its tenth hour. We take the first exit, hop a high-security fence, and traverse a field of sagebrush toward the confluence. Joe's limp drags as we drop into the backyard of a suburban home where a woman watches Fox News, something about Donald Trump's rise. Clean coal. Fake news. Passing the Chinese buffet where Joe and I first met, a chef sits on his haunches sucking on the glowing nub of a Lucky Strike. Joe's whole face smiles as he calls Sherry to let her know we're alive. "We're home!" he says. I find myself envious of his commitment to this home, despite its overwhelming toxicity. But maybe that's what makes a home worth living in, to turn toward both its beauty and its trauma, to hold them in the same animal heart, and to have the staying power to endure.

"We've gotta own this pit," Joe says to me. "It's not going anywhere. It's a commitment, but we have to own it now." The two of us walk single file along a busy frontage road. "I've made my whole living off this pit, so I see it as a sort of sacred act at this point." He looks out at the city. "Man, I'm excited about Butte. There is a total repackaging going on here. Folk festival is world-class. Art scene picking up. Great mountain biking and cross-country skiing. Young people trying to make a life out here. It's just such a beautiful location, I mean look around!"

I swivel around and still cannot fully understand. To my right is one of the largest humanmade toxic holes on Earth. To my left, shelves of coal-colored slag piled twenty feet high. And underfoot, ten thousand miles of poisoned shafts swimming with ghosts. I catch a glimpse of the Anselmo headframe in the distance and remember the charred men underground in the 1917 fire, the worker riots, Frank Little hanging bloated from a railroad trestle. There are so many reasons to hate this place. I find myself in a cycle of revulsion-escapism again, turning from a place, or a Self, replete with trauma, razed forests and boiling seas and choked air. How do I come back to a planet in equivalent disrepair? How do I come home to a place I've never left? The Pit's invitation is subtle: *Don't look away. Come closer. Slow down. Look beneath. Now get to work.*

We had walked twenty miles around the country's largest Superfund site, and Joe remains allegiant to keeping this place alive as best he can, for to turn away now is to disavow a violation that is of our own making. To steward what beauty remains, to protect ecological functions into perpetuity, requires us to face this damage head-on and flag each misstep along the way so it never bears repeating. Escape is no longer an option; there is nowhere else to go. The Japanese poet, Shinkichi Takahashi, born on Shikoku Island, site of a thousand-mile, eighty-eight-temple Zen circumambulation, wrote:

> The wind blows hard among the pines
> Toward the beginning
> Of an endless past.
> Listen: you've heard everything.

We've set into motion what Joanna Macy calls the Great Unraveling, where everything has now begun to whip faster, unraveling at the seams, and what's needed most is to slow the spin, to rein back the pace of attendance, back into the Earth's animate blood-rich core through proximity and radical acts of subversive presence. Here, the Pit reveals its task: Hold the center together with the pressing of your dumb feet. Bow to the unconquerable mountain. Land reflects the lies we've told ourselves, those of progress, modernity, linearity, bigger and faster and newer and take it and rip it and own it. Listen: A song of dissent rises with these dark waters, an ecology of mutualism and innumerable acts of bravery tended to at every level. Look: Everywhere desacralized places bleed in broad daylight, even as there remains resistance and stewardship, those committed to flourishing. See: Radical is rooted and rooted is intimacy in walking alongside a place or person long enough to honor all of their sides, even the shadowy toxic sides, because the winds, the tides, the fires, they're all picking up now—our roots are being tested.

"Life is a self-evolving circle, which, from a ring imperceptibly small, rushes on all sides outward to new and larger circles, and that without end," writes Ralph Waldo Emerson in "Circles," his 1841 essay. "The extent to which this generation of circles, wheel without wheel, will go, depends on the force or truth of the individual soul." The poet-essayist considers the circle a primary shape that starts with the eye, with seeing, our optical-perceptual witness tasked with widening and deepening its gaze. "Our life is an apprenticeship to the truth, that around every circle another can be drawn; that there is no end in nature, but every end is a beginning." Around each circle another can be drawn, that the circumference etched around our overcivilized selves will one day prove myopic, apertures not dilated enough by sun or shadow or curiosity or love for the world to receive much beyond familiar dimensions of the Self.

"Everything looks permanent until its secret is known," writes Emerson, in poetic dialogue with something Robert Frost wrote: "We dance round in a ring and suppose, / But the Secret sits in the middle and knows." The ineffable, the mystery, is what must be centered. That is, unless the secret itself is impermanence, and modern life is one more crude attempt to capture a sense of permanence in the face of incomprehensible mortality, and all our human quibbling, all our institutions and relationships and loves and wars and babies and bombs, are responses to some ultimate psychic terror of disappearance, and because it's far too big to hold at once, we aim straight ahead and take what we can as fast as we can, moving and consuming too fast for our bodies to catch up. But now, the Earth body is catching up.

"Everything is medial," Emerson writes. Everything is central. Each one of our thoughts is built by ripples of circumstance, and from there a crust forms, a berm to "hem in the life." Emerson intimates that our job is to constantly "burst over that boundary," to expand beyond our personal circumference to inhabit "another orbit on the great deep," which will inevitably rub against yet another boundary of this evolution through revolution.

"The heart refuses to be imprisoned . . . it already tends outward with a vast force, and to immense and innumerable expansions." We further inhabit these widening contours of belonging as long as we continue to look, the eye being our primary circle of invitation, attention to see our own divinity.

"There is no outside, no inclosing wall, no circumference to us," writes Emerson. A walk without destination confirms this route to wholeness as something nonlinear, a table without a head, a counterpoint to prevailing Western primacy of the self as center. "No virtue is final," he writes. "All are initial. We must cast away our virtues into the same pit that has consumed our grosser vices," thus signaling life's central tension, an "incessant movement and progression" contrasted with some "principle of fixture or stability in soul."

Emerson argues that "whilst the eternal generation of circles proceeds, the eternal generator abides," that within each life's orbit is a blueprint for how best to arrive at the next circle of belonging. Its invitation whispers through the everyday—in relationship, in solitude, through poetry, journals, observation, and protest. If we were to stop circling, then we halt such interest in enlarging our coliseum of identity to include all living things. A dyke will form around our heart, stunting participation with a world we know to be possible.

At the end of the essay, what Emerson suggests is the following: Life's eddies are invitations for widening circles of actualized life, insofar as we stay awake, insofar as we keep looking with unending wonder. "The total growths and universal movements of the soul, he hideth; they are incalculable," he writes. Perhaps this is what I crave most: to lose myself through this kind of devotion, an aspirational pilgriming into union, an endurance event that merges me with what I inherently know to already be mine, remembered through a surrender "to forget ourselves, to be surprised out of our own propriety ... in short, to draw a new circle."

...

Joe and I reach the confluence of Silver Bow and Blacktail Creeks after having drawn a new circle, and violet skies meet our arrival. My feet squish with blisters as Joe pulls out his canteen and walks to where the two creeks collide. Here is a person who reflects this very place: someone converged and conflicted, industrial conspirator and citizen protectorate. Joe squats by the water's edge, closes his eyes, takes a deep breath as sun glitters off the creek's surface to fill his canister with diamonds of light. Willow and alder bend closer to witness as minnows stir in eddies below, stroking new life. Joe opens his eyes to dump the water into the creek, and the offering ripples outward. I think of Pierre's release at Lake Manasarovar. I think of Laura's piercing eyes on the northern flank of Mount Tamalpais. I think of my mother's parchment-paper cheek. To walk around a pit, bushwhacking past surveillance cameras and warning signs telling us not to continue, but to go anyway and fetch a jar of wild water and walk it around to the present, to irrigate an unknown future, is carrying both pleasure and pain, renewal and extinction.

Now it's my turn. I pour my bottle into the stream, watch as it's taken in by the headwaters, and our mission is complete. The circle is unbroken, mending something for one shimmering, inconsequential moment. I realized that to come down from the mountain is to instead walk slowly alongside these complicated and unanswerable ecotones of grief, wonder, and humility. I've only begun to move around this interior place.

Endings feed beginnings. May I release the summit. May I set down this imperial hardware and move along my own circumference with stubborn endurance and surrender, driven by humility, compassion, and staying power. Maybe it's all too late to retrieve what's been lost in all our take, but that doesn't deflect the central task of the circumambulator: to find embodied practice that resituates humans not as center, but as one of innumerable centers of gravity in this moment—Earth dethroned as center of the universe, humans dethroned to relinquish their gaudy headdress and feed it back to the pitted source as an offering and a homecoming. This is the way around, I'm learning, to follow these rounds until our crown spins from arrogance and toward honesty, to reciprocity, choosing routes and shapes that bring us most alive and that direct us back to nowhere and everywhere, toward the familiarity of a beginning that never ends.

The sun is down. I look around for a sign, for that great blue heron to flap her wings in affirmation, but nothing so poetic arrives. Instead, I offer the primary circles of my eyes as witness to the ripples that continue to widen and meet the creek's edge before dispersing downstream toward some new beginning. Joe and I embrace. His shirt smells of an endless wind.

EPILOGUE

Then I was standing on the highest mountain of them all, and round about beneath me was the whole hoop of the world. And while I stood there I saw more than I can tell and understood more than I saw; for I was seeing in a sacred manner the shapes of all things in the spirit, and the shape of all shapes as they must live together like one being. And I saw that the sacred hoop of my people was one of many hoops that made one circle, wide as daylight and as starlight, and in the center grew one mighty flowering tree to shelter all the children of one mother and one father. And I saw that it was holy. But anywhere is the center of the world.

—Black Elk

It's June 2024, and I am standing at the finish line of the Western States 100-Mile Endurance Run, watching as my younger self enters onto the high school track in Auburn, California, for a victory lap set to cheers from the crowd. I follow this twenty-eight-year-old me as he sprints with an unsettled expression on his face, one of pride and defeat, conquest and surrender, accomplishment and failure. He curls around the last bend as hamstrings seize up, spittle comes from his mouth, and dried blood covers both kneecaps. He arrives to the end of the single biggest commitment of his life. Reaching, always reaching.

When he reaches the finish line, a hundred miles and nearly nineteen hours later, I imagine the two of us squaring up eye to eye, before he collapses into a heap of exhaustion after pile driving his body into the ground in a nonstop search for something forever outside himself. I join him there at ground level, lying beside his rank puddle of gore, wiping caked salt from his face, removing the sweat-encrusted hat from his head, embracing his sunburned body to say, "You are enough."

After two decades of tracking the art of circuitous pilgrimage around the world, I keep returning to this moment as a pivotal point in the story, an end of the longest race of my life and also the beginning of the adventure that unfolded. This was the moment that required something to break, to rupture and die, and for the devotion to a different story, a new shape, to begin. I can see now why that needed to happen, how such extreme pummeling forward without end can force the body to confront how unconscious we've become in pursuing the never-to-be-reached, and how this hardened mentality was part of a larger cultural myth, the myth of the never-enough striving that shaped every step.

As my body fell apart at that finish line, so too is the Earth body. This planet has long been flashing warning signals that the modern industrial culture of human-first domination and hyperefficiency comes at the fatal cost of a planet unraveling at unprecedented speed. For us to continue firing ahead at such a pace, at a cadence disconnected from these entangled bodies of knowing, is to continue imagining humans as the only possible hero in this story, a planetary peak-bagger, only for us to reach a summit and look down upon a desecrated landscape of our own undoing. This is no peak. This is a mirror.

To square the circle. Perhaps I've been courting the opposite this whole time, a circling of the square, desperate to strike out in another direction than the one modern life constantly demanded of me. Of course, the literal shape of circuitous movement was never really the thing, more the process and relational field of compassion and attention that unfolded along the path. The act of circumambulation, I found, invited me to relate in radically different ways to landscape, and to myself, to being further sculpted by place as well as people—awe and grief, belonging and loss, restraint and revelation. By slowing the pace and not fixating on arrival, I've become more aware of the dominant cultural shapes directing my life and found courage to inhabit different routes of mind that bore more honest resemblance to what and how I actually wished to live.

This process, like the shape itself, will never end.

How do the shapes we follow shape us? How do the stories we follow shape how we relate to the world, to ourselves, to Other, to God? These continue to be my guiding questions, questions with no answer in sight, a mountain without a summit—my favorite kind. The way around isn't revealed as some buttoned-up counternarrative to imperial linearity or "king of the mountain" hegemony. I've found it to be something far smaller and more spell-casting than that. These routes have reshaped how I relate to my own capacity as witness, attendant to subtlety, and steward to the mess we've made, and how to step into a more devotional and resilient shape, one that forges new generative ways of beauty out of circumstance. Even the word *circumstance* includes its prefix *circum-*, which itself has shape, relating to "being encompassing," or to "make or be firm in a surrounding condition." This journey offered me a way into the very heart of circumstance, holding multiple truths in the same body at once with emergent grace, to learn that these routes we follow are always multivalent, and yet they always dictate our ways of seeing and being, so we better choose our way with care. And this might be the most important task of all: finding courage not to escape or evade the increasing torque of violence toward planet and people through further distraction or numbing, automation or accumulation, but rather to face the coming storm as our own, both its screaming tempest at the edge and also the calm eye in the center.

We are both center and circumference.

We are the center of the mountain, and so is everything else.

As I lie here at midnight with my previous self, puddled there together on that synthetic rubber track that smells of petroleum under bright lights and cheers and music, I meditate on the patterned heave of his chest, the rising and falling with great velocity. So fast, I think. Too fast. Eventually it slows, and I try for a moment to pair my beating heart with his, try and work as one body to slow this spin and come back home to the pace of enough. I imagine holding him as we breathe together, right there at the finish line in this shape of collapse, both of us, all of us, pilgrims going nowhere. I am learning to embrace these parts of us we can't let go of easily, the reaching, forever-seeking parts that continue to strain outside ourselves for love and belonging, inducing a kind of perpetual homelessness. I have no option but to step into another lap, and another, asking endlessly with my feet for guidance, held in orbit by some renewable energy source far older and slower and more patient, an unknowable, wild divinity spinning its yarn of endless song, the shape of homecoming to a place we've never left.

NOTES

ix   **Mystics claim that** Jorge Luis Borges, "The Library of Babel," in *Labyrinths*, trans. James E. Irby and Donald A. Yates (New Directions, 1962), 113.

Prologue

1   **I live my life** Rainer Maria Rilke, "Widening Circles," *Book of Hours: Love Poems to God*, trans. Joanna Macy and Anita Burrows (Riverhead, 2005), 45.

Round One: Kailash

11   **Starlings circle in the sky** James Baldwin, "Munich, Winter 1973 (for Y.S.)," in *Jimmy's Blues and Other Poems* (Beacon, 2014).

21   **Kailash is a mountain** Ippolito Desideri, *An Account of Tibet: The Travels of Ippolito Desideri of Pistoia, S.J. 1712-1727*, ed. Filippo De Filippi (Routledge, 2004).

21   **At every turn** Sven Hedin, *Trans-Himalaya: Discoveries and Adventures in Tibet*, 3 vols. (Macmillan, 1910), 192.

22   **Only a man entirely free** Nyima Samkar, *Mount Kailash: The White Mirror* (Library of Tibetan Works and Archives, 2020).

22   **If we conquer this mountain** Samkar, *Mount Kailash*.

25   ***Completely false." Baker claimed***   Ian Baker quoted by Ian Baker. Joshua Hammer, "Baker in the Palace with the Statuette," *Outside* online, September 1, 2008, https://www.outsideonline.com/adventure-travel/destinations/asia/baker-palace-statuette/.

28   ***the walking god***   "Litany of Ra," I, 62, 72; II, 17, in *The Records of the Past* (Forgotten Books, 2018), 8:111.

28   ***Thou stridest over the heaven***   *The Egyptian Book of the Dead,* trans. E.A. Wallis Budge (Kegan Paul, Trench, Trubner & Co., Ltd., 1898), 33.

41   ***medieval pain-helmet***   Robert Macfarlane, *The Old Ways* (Penguin, 2013), 274.

45   ***Behold, we gave***   "Aya al-Hajj" ("The Pilgrimage"), in the Qur'an, trans. Muhammad Marmaduke Pickthall and Mohammad Abdul Haleem Eliase (Rightway, 1999), 22:26.

48   ***I noticed… a moving***   Alexandra David-Néel, *Magic and Mystery in Tibet* (Dover, 1971).

49   ***Immense herds of kiang***   The Dalai Lama, "The Natural World," *His Holiness the 14th Dalai Lama of Tibet*, accessed October 22, 2024, https://www.dalailama.com/messages/environment/the-natural-world.

49   ***Somewhere in these wilds***   Colin Thubron, *To a Mountain in Tibet* (Harper Perennial, 2011), 159.

50   ***Wanting to drain***   Robert A. F. Thurman and Tad Wise, *Circling the Sacred Mountain: A Spiritual Adventure Through the Himalayas* (Bantam, 1999), 263.

57   ***Be united. Study Tibetan culture***   Rikyo, who self-immolated on October 9, 2014. These lines are from her testament to her family. Tibetan Youth

Round Two: Tamalpais

	Congress, accessed October 24, 2024, https://www.tibetanyouthcongress.org/40-rikyo/.	

61   *There is much*   Herman Melville, *Moby Dick* (Penguin, 2013), 254.

63   *They know our sort*   Gary Snyder, *Passage Through India* (Counterpoint, 1972), 12.

63   *Next to the site*   Snyder, *Passage*, 20.

63   *day and night*   Snyder, *Passage*, 51.

64   *The personality of a mountain*   Lama Anagarika Govinda, *The Way of the White Clouds: A Buddhist Pilgrim in Tibet* (Shambhala, 1970), 271–272.

66   *Walking up and around*   Gary Snyder, "The Circumambulation of Mount Tamalpais," in *Mountains and Rivers Without End* (Counterpoint, 1996), 87–91.

70   *I didn't really know*   Tom Killion and Gary Snyder, *Tamalpais Walking* (Heyday, 2009), 108–109.

72   *if you didn't realize*   Joseph Campbell and Bill Moyers in conversation. *The Power of Myth*, episode 2, "The Message of the Myth," aired June 22, 1988, and episode 3, "The First Storytellers," aired June 23, 1988, on PBS, https://billmoyers.com/series/joseph-campbe ll-and-the-power-of-myth-1988/.

74   *Praises gentle Tamalpais*   Lew Welch, *Ring of Bone: Collected Poems, 1950-1971* (Grey Fox, 1973).

79   *the finest book ever written*   Nicholas Lezard, review of *The Living Mountain* by Nan Shepherd, *The Guardian*, September 20, 2011, https://www.theguardian.com/books/2011/sep/20/living-mountain-nan-shepherd-review.

79 *I am on a plateau again* Nan Shepherd, *The Living Mountain* (Canongate, 2011), 22.
79 *The pilgrim contents herself* Robert Macfarlane's introduction. Shepherd, *The Living Mountain*, xvii.
79 *Often the mountain gives* Shepherd, *The Living Mountain*, 15.
80 *I now understand* Shepherd, *The Living Mountain*, 108.
85 *It is guarded by the Demon* George Band, "The Conquest of Kanchenjunga," *Sports Illustrated*, October 3, 1955, https://vault.si.com/vault/1955/10/03/the-conquest-of-kanchenjunga.
86 *It would be like climbing* Chris Kalman, "It's Time to Rethink Devil's Tower," *Outside* online, July 25, 2018, https://www.outsideonline.com/outdoor-adventure/climbing/why-its-time-rethink-climbing-ban-devils-tower/.
87 *Night after night* Ruth M. Underhill, *Singing for Power: The Song Magic of the Papago Indians of Southern Arizona* (University of Arizona Press, 1993).
87 *It is a bad way to live* Black Elk and John G. Neihardt, *Black Elk Speaks* (University of Nebraska Press, 1979), 150.
91 *Allah, Allah, Allah* Original source unknown. Jedidiah Rumi, "Turkey's Whirling Dervish Guide to Coping with Pain and a Broken Heart," May 21, 2019, https://www.cnn.com/2019/05/17/health/chasing-life-turkey-whirling-dervish-pain-broken-heart/index.html.
92 *I'm goin to Marin County* Jack Kerouac, *The Dharma Bums* (Penguin, 1976), 101.

94 **Human events and the course** Bernard Cohen, *Revolution in Science* (Belknap, 1987).
94 **No beginning could be made** Hannah Arendt, *On Revolution* (Penguin, 2006), 10.
95 **One of our finest methods** Ursula K. Le Guin, "A Non-Euclidean View of California," Yale Review, December 1, 1983, https://yalereview.org/article/ursula-le-guin-non-euclidean-view.
95 **the stars follow** Hannah Arendt, *On Revolution* (Penguin, 2006), 30–48.
95 **Life itself is revolutionary** Thomas Merton, *Disputed Questions* (Mariner, 1985).
96 **Any worldview that makes sense** Paul Kingsnorth, "The Witness," in *Confessions of a Recovering Environmentalist and Other Essays* (Graywolf, 2017), 221.
105 **To the Summit** Philip Whalen, "Opening the Mountain: Tamalpais: 22:x:65," in *On Bear's Head* (Harcourt, 1969), 307–308.
106 **its base must be very broad** René Daumal, *Mount Analogue: A Novel of Symbolically Authentic Non-Euclidean Adventures in Mountain Climbing*, trans. Roger Shattuck (Exact Change, 2019), 73.
107 **The landscape abounds** William deBuys, *The Walk* (Trinity University Press, 2007), 13.
108 **A dispassionate observer** deBuys, *The Walk*, 7.
110 **And when you have reached** Kahlil Gibran, "On Death," in *The Prophet* (Knopf, 1965).
112 **A way to see the mountain** Tom Killion and Gary Snyder, *Tamalpais Walking* (Heyday, 2009), 41.
119 **Perhaps the most radical thing** Rebecca Solnit, "The Most Radical Thing You Can Do," *Orion*,

October 21, 2008, https://orionmagazine.org/article/the-most-radical-thing-you-can-do/.

ROUND THREE: PIT

123 **The wind blows hard** Shinkichi Takahashi, "Wind among the Pines," in *Triumph of the Sparrow: Zen Poems of Shinkichi Takahashi*, trans. Lucien Stryk (Grove, 2007).

131 **When the goldfinch** Antonio Machado, "[Traveler, your footprints]," in *There Is No Road*, trans. by Mary G. Berg and Dennis Maloney (White Pine, 2003).

135 **Grant will encircle Lee's forces** Horace Greeley, referenced by John Neilsen. "From Mine to Consumer: The Anaconda Copper Company," *Mining Artifact Collector*, Spring 1993, https://mineralogicalrecord.com/wp-content/uploads/2023/12/HISTORY-Neilson-Anaconda-Copper-Co.-MAC-18-SPRING-1993.pdf.

136 **expectation of imminent abandonment** Michael Punke, *Fire and Brimstone: The North Butte Mining Disaster of 1917* (Hyperion, 2006), 87.

145 **security collar fixed to the neck** Iain Sinclair, *London Orbital* (Penguin, 2002), 11.

145 **The circuits become** Sinclair, *London Orbital*, 347.

146 **As the sun travels** Sinclair is quoting Dr. Dylan Francis from an essay titled "William Harvey and the 'Motion in a Circle,'" Sinclair, *London Orbital*, 256.

146 **All walks contradict the lie** Sinclair, *London Orbital*, 43.

147 **It's [enough] to keep our head** Quoting Butte resident Kristen Ryan. Chris McGreal, "Financial Despair, Addition, and the Rise of Suicide in

America," *The Guardian*, February 7, 2016, https://www.theguardian.com/us-news/2016/feb/07/suicide-rates-rise-butte-montana-princeton-study.

148   **The words I often see** McGreal, "Financial Despair."
156   **I began to understand** Carl Jung, *Memories, Dreams, Reflections* (Harper Perennial/Fontana, 1995), 222. Originally published by Random House in German, 1961.
157   **To Indigenous, oral cultures** David Abram, *The Spell of the Sensuous* (First Vintage, 1997), 185.
158   **find oneself in a world** Abram, *The Spell*, 186.
159   **I followed the line** Nonprofit journalism about criminal justice. Tracy Meadows, "The Big Chill," in *Life Inside, The Marshall Project*, November 29, 2018, https://www.themarshallproject.org/2018/11/29/the-big-chill.
165   **Life is a self-evolving circle** Ralph Waldo Emerson, "Circles," in *Selected Essays, Lectures, and Poems* (Bantam Classic, 1990), 193–204.
166   **We dance round in a ring** Robert Frost, "The Secret Sits," original publication unknown.

Epilogue

171   **Then I was standing** Black Elk and John G. Neihardt, *Black Elk Speaks* (University of Nebraska Press, 1979), 33.

ADDITIONAL SOURCES
SELECTED FURTHER READING

Alison, Jane. *Meander, Spiral, Explore: Design and Pattern in Narrative.* Catapult, 2019.
Baker, J. A. *The Peregrine.* New York Review of Books, 1967.
Bateson, Nora. *Small Arcs of Larger Circles: Framing Through Other Patterns.* Triarchy Press, 2016.
Chaplin, Joyce E. *Round About the Earth: Circumnavigation from Magellan to Orbit.* Simon & Schuster, 2012.
Chatwin, Bruce. *The Songlines.* Penguin Books, 1987.
D'Agata, John. *About a Mountain.* W. W. Norton & Co., 2010.
Dillard, Annie. *Pilgrim at Tinker Creek.* Harper's Magazine Press, 1974.
Hoelting, Kurt. *The Circumference of Home.* Da Capo Press, 2010.
Hogan, Linda. *Dwellings: A Spiritual History of the Living World.* W. W. Norton & Co., 1995.
Huxley, Aldous. *The Perennial Philosophy.* Harper Perennial, 1945.
Lane, John. *Circling Home.* University of Georgia Press, 2009.
Lima, Manuel. *The Book of Circles: Visualizing Spheres of Knowledge.* Princeton Architectural Press, 2017.
Macfarlane, Robert. *Mountains of the Mind: Adventures in Reaching the Summit.* Vintage Books, 2003.
Plotkin, Bill. *Nature and the Human Soul: Cultivating Wholeness and Community in a Fragmented World.* New World Press, 2008.
Sebald, W. G. *The Rings of Saturn.* New Directions, 1979.
Silko, Leslie Marmon. *Ceremony.* Penguin Books, 1977.
Solnit, Rebecca. *A Field Guide to Getting Lost.* Penguin Books, 2005.
Solnit, Rebecca. *The Faraway Nearby.* Viking, 2013.
Solnit, Rebecca. *Wanderlust: A History of Walking.* Penguin Books, 2001.

Tanahashi, Kazuaki and Peter Levitt. *The Essential Dogen: Writings of the Great Zen Master.* Shambhala, 2013.

Tsing, Anna Lowenhaupt. *The Mushroom at the End of the World: On the Possibility of Life in Capitalist Ruins.* Princeton University Press, 2015.

Whitman, Walt. *Leaves of Grass.* Dover Publications, 2007. Originally by the author, 1855.

Winn, Raynor. *The Salt Path.* Penguin Books, 2018.

Yunkaporta, Tyson. *Sand Talk: How Indigenous Thinking Can Save the World.* Harper One, 2020.

Round One: Kailash

Baker, Ian. *The Heart of the World.* Penguin Books, 2006.

Buckley, Michael. *Meltdown in Tibet: China's Reckless Destruction of Ecosystems from the Highlands of Tibet to the Deltas of Asia.* Palgrave Macmillan, 2014.

Demick, Barbara. *Eat the Buddha: Life and Death in a Tibetan Town.* Random House, 2020.

Ellsworth, Scott. *The World Beneath Their Feet: Mountaineering, Madness, and the Race to Summit the Himalayas.* Little, Brown, and Co., 2020.

Gillette, Ned and Jan Reynolds. *Everest Grand Circle.* Mountaineers Books, 1985.

Ives, Katie. *Imaginary Peaks: The Riesenstein Hoax and Other Mountain Dreams.* Mountaineers Books, 2021.

Raguin, Virginia C. and Dina Bangdel. *Pilgrimage and Faith.* Serindia Publications, 2010.

Round Two: Tamalpais

Gibson, Jack. *Mount Tamalpais and the Marin Municipal Water District.* Arcadia Publishing, 2012.

Goerke, Betty. *Chief Marin: Leader, Rebel, and Legend: A History of Marin County's Namesake and His People.* Heyday, 2007.

Gonnerman, Mark. *A Sense of the Whole: Reading Gary Snyder's Mountains and Rivers Without End.* Counterpoint, 2015.

Fairley, Lincoln. *Mount Tamalpais: A History.* Scottwall, 1987.

Halper, Jon. *Gary Snyder: Dimensions of a Life*. Sierra Club Books, 1991.
Margolin, Malcolm. *The Ohlone Way: Indian Life in the San Francisco-Monterey Bay Area*. Heyday, 1978.
Snyder, Gary. *Regarding Wave*. New Directions, 1967.
Snyder, Gary. *The Practice of the Wild*. North Point Press, 1990.
Snyder, Gary. *The Real Work: Interviews & Talks 1964-1979*. New Directions, 1980.
Suiter, John. *Poets on the Peaks: Gary Snyder, Philip Whalen, and Jack Kerouac in the North Cascades*. Counterpoint, 2002.
White, Micah. *The End of Protest: A New Playbook for Revolution*. Knopf Canada, 2016.

Round Three: Pit

Dobb, Edwin. "Pennies from Hell." *Harper's*. October 1996.
Doig, Ivan. *Sweet Thunder*. Riverhead Books, 2013.
Gibson, Richard I. *Lost Butte Montana*. History Press, 2012.
Leech, Brian James. *The City That Ate Itself: Butte*. University of Nevada Press, 2018.
MacLane, Mary. *I Await the Devil's Coming*. Melville House, 2013.

ACKNOWLEDGMENTS

To fully and appropriately express my gratitude for everyone that went into making this project happen would be an impossible feat, but I'll try. First, I'd like to begin by expressing thanks to the landscapes and the communities I visited in writing *The Way Around*. To have the access and the available means to traverse Tibet, to walk the paths around Tamalpais, and explore the gash of the Berkeley Pit means to also confront and be in relationship with these traditional lands, and that my trespass and passage is both conflicted and honored. In Kailash, special thanks to Ian Baker for his generosity in inviting me on his journey, and for sharing so much of his kaleidoscopic intelligence about the region, *kora*, and Buddhism. To Pierre, your eccentric, compassionate heart has been a constant battery for me, since meeting in 2014. Thanks for opening to me. The whole group was a special one, and I've been blessed to still be in close touch with Nym, Yvan, and Macy, and am thankful for your friendship and trust in telling this story. Rodney Smith passed in 2020, and I dedicate the Kailash part to his enduring spirit.

For the Tamalpais portion, I cannot thank Laura Pettibone and her wonderful wife, Anne, enough for sharing their lives with me. Laura passed away in 2022, and this book is dedicated to her level of devotion—to the walk, to the mountain, and to her courageous heart. She's surely dancing on a cliff edge right now and taking the lead. Special thanks to Mike Scott, John Lane, Kazuaki Tanahashi, Michael Branch, and Rebecca Solnit for consultation and inspiration. Special thanks also to Vance and Nancy Carruth of Jackson Hole, Wyoming, for creating a writing residency for me as an extension of the Murie Writers Residency, but you both believed in my project. I wrote the entire first draft of the Tamalpais chapter in your daughter's bedroom.

In Butte, my deep thanks to Joe and Sherry Griffin for the handful of visits, an overnight, and the many phone calls. Thank you for entrusting your wonderful home and life with me. And a shoutout to Nora Saks, journalist and podcast host of *Butte, America*, who helped read early drafts and shared whiskey in Butte.

The incubator that gave rise to this whole idea was the University of Montana's environmental writing graduate program, and I have to thank Phil Condon for seeing something in my work, something that perhaps I didn't even see, and giving me a chance. Also, Dan Spencer and the UM EVST faculty, which includes visiting writers and mentors Janisse Ray, William deBuys, David James Duncan, Chris Dombrowski, and Amy Irvine, all of whom changed what I knew to be possible in my own work. And to my cohort of writers: Trevien Stanger, Emily Withnall (*Camas Magazine* co-editor), Colin May, Heather Griffith, Mel Wardlow, Chandra Brown, Kathleen Tarrant, Emma Duke, Caroline Stephens, Chris Reed, Jolene Brink, Nick Littman, Kate Stanley, Oliver Wood, and Megan McInerney, for stomaching early drafts and providing real critical feedback. Thanks to Kerri Rosenstein for showing me what it means to be a real artist, and to Zoë Rom, Brian Metzler, and all my editorial comrades at *Outside* and *Trail Runner*. I learned so much for your ambition and creative endurance.

My colleagues during my time at *Orion* magazine, Sumanth Prabhaker, Katie Yale, Madeline Miller, and Chip Blake, all helped by popping the hood on what makes for proper writing. And while we're in New England, dear literary foot-traveler friends Daegan Miller, Jason Sarouhan, Sheldon Snodgrass, and Matt Ferrari were subjected to hours of on-trail ideation workshopping for honing the major concepts in this book. Since 2019, I've been part of a small group of writers called The Curling Club. Meeting every month with you three—Kitty Galloway, Micah Sewell, and Alex Carr Johnson—has turned into an evening I look forward to each month, accountability as we all wade into the deep end of our creative selves. Thank you for making that space safe and expansive to be myself—and for reading a lot of crap drafts.

And to the fine folks at Milkweed Editions, I couldn't have asked for a better fit for this project and am indebted to Daniel Slager for giving me a chance, and to Helen Whybrow for helping me along with such patience and compassion in its earlier phases. Most importantly, I'd like to thank my family. Aunt Geegee, I wouldn't be here without you, full stop. Ryan, your intelligence and consistency offered a stabilizing buoy through all of this, whether you know it or not. Dad, you've been there as my life's crew chief at every single bend in the path, every race, every phone call. Your unwavering encouragement for travel, for writing, for outdoor pursuit with a conscience, set me up for seeing our world through humble eyes and a strong heart. And Mom, I love you more than words can express. I owe you everything. This is for you.

NICHOLAS TRIOLO is a writer, filmmaker, photographer, activist, and long-distance trail runner. His writing and images have been featured in *Orion*, *Outside*, the Dark Mountain Project, and *Trail Runner*, and on Terrain.org. He has directed two documentary films, *The Crossing* and *Shaped by Fire*, and collaborated with Salomon on a film about touring and training Death Cab for Cutie frontman Ben Gibbard. Triolo's films have been Official Selections for several international film festivals and featured on influential platforms such as Patagonia's Dirtbag Diaries, Upworthy, and *Outside*. Triolo is based in Missoula, Montana, and you can read more about him at nicholastriolo.net.

milkweed
EDITIONS

Founded as a nonprofit organization in 1980, Milkweed Editions is an independent publisher. Our mission is to identify, nurture, and publish transformative literature, and build an engaged community around it.

We are based in Bde Óta Othúŋwe (Minneapolis) in Mní Sota Makhóčhe (Minnesota), the traditional homeland of the Dakhóta and Anishinaabe (Ojibwe) people and current home to many thousands of Dakhóta, Ojibwe, and other Indigenous people, including four federally recognized Dakhóta nations and seven federally recognized Ojibwe nations.

We believe all flourishing is mutual, and we envision a future in which all can thrive. Realizing such a vision requires reflection on historical legacies and engagement with current realities. We humbly encourage readers to do the same.

milkweed.org

Milkweed Editions, an independent nonprofit literary publisher, gratefully acknowledges sustaining support from our board of directors, the McKnight Foundation, the National Endowment for the Arts, and many generous contributions from foundations, corporations, and thousands of individuals—our readers. This activity is made possible by the voters of Minnesota through a Minnesota State Arts Board Operating Support grant, thanks to a legislative appropriation from the Arts and Cultural Heritage Fund.

Interior design by Mike Corrao
Typeset in Bely

Bely was designed by Roxane Gataud for the TypeTogether foundry in 2014. Bely is designed with classical proportions for maximum legibility and received the Type Directors Club Award of Excellence in Type Design in 2017.